ARGYLE

A YEAR IN MY LIFE AS A
PARK RANGER

WAYNE W. WHITE

Copyright © 2019 Wayne W. White.

All rights reserved. No part of this book may be reproduced, stored, or transmitted by any means—whether auditory, graphic, mechanical, or electronic—without written permission of the author, except in the case of brief excerpts used in critical articles and reviews. Unauthorized reproduction of any part of this work is illegal and is punishable by law.

This book is a work of non-fiction. Unless otherwise noted, the author and the publisher make no explicit guarantees as to the accuracy of the information contained in this book and in some cases, names of people and places have been altered to protect their privacy.

ISBN: 978-1-4834-9885-0 (sc)
ISBN: 978-1-4834-9357-2 (e)

Because of the dynamic nature of the Internet, any web addresses or links contained in this book may have changed since publication and may no longer be valid. The views expressed in this work are solely those of the author and do not necessarily reflect the views of the publisher, and the publisher hereby disclaims any responsibility for them.

Any people depicted in stock imagery provided by Getty Images are models, and such images are being used for illustrative purposes only.
Certain stock imagery © Getty Images.

Lulu Publishing Services rev. date: 08/05/2019

CONTENTS

Dedication ix
Preface xi
Introduction xiii
Winter 1
    Snow Storm 4
    Winter Emergency 5
    Snowmobiles 5
    Christmas Tree Pickup 6
    Boy Scouts Campout 7
    Not Enough Paint 7
    Ranger Meeting In Springfield 8
    Helping The Sheriff 10
    Catastrophe Averted 10
    Icy Hills 11
    Vacation 11
    Camp Ground Hosts 12
    Concessionere 13
Spring 15
    Summer Help 16
    The Zoo 18
    Becky & Agnes 22
    Millie The Pony 24
    Easter 25
    The Chapel 26
    Spring Flora 27

    Memorial Day Weekend 31
    Tree Cutting 32
    The Wood Chipper 32
    College Kids Vs Townies 33
    The Gordy Taylor Story 34
    The Terrible Storm 35

Summer 37
    The Beavers 38
    The Coal Mine 38
    Death In The Campground 40
    Picnics And Reunions 41
    Fishing 43
    Little Fisherman 44
    Pontoons 48
    Help From The Game Wardens 52
    Gypsies 53
    Hot Air Balloon Ride 54
    Iron Axmen 56
    Aqua Clowns 56
    Diver Training 57
    Political Maneuvers 57
    Silting Of The Lake 59
    The Adkinson Cemetery 61
    Missing Boy 63
    Campers 63
    WIU Theatre Program 64
    The Windmill 64
    Squirrel Hunters 64
    Rainy Sunday 65
    Local Bikers 66
    Scare While Moving Pontoon 68
    A Visit From Trooper Hocker 69
    Wizard Of Play 72
    Log Cabin 75
    WIU Dorm Reunion 75
    Speaking Engagements 76

Last Day For C.E.T.A. Workers 76
Rugby 81
Bass Tournament 81
Swimmers At The Docks 82
Child Left Behind 83
Horseshoe Tournament 83
Working At The State Fair 84
Dry Leaves Cause Fire 86
Labor Day 88
Rugby Tournament 90
Cutting Wheat 90
Labor Day Vendors 91
Naturalist Hired 92
Setting Up On Friday 93
Happy Birthday Smokey The Bear 98
Saturday of Labor Day Weekend 100
Sunday of Labor Day Weekend 102
Gas Engine Club 103

Fall 107
Fire In The Woods 108
Road Resurfacing 109
Helping Out A Neighbor 110
Class Trips In The Fall 110
What Were They Doing? 112
Make Me Smile 112
A One Time Square Dance 114
The Lost Ring 114
Pulling The Plug 115
Another Rugby Tournament 115
Archery Range 117
Pontoon Jumpers 117
A Sign For The Dorm 117
Public Service 118
River Ride 118
Trout Release 119
Fishing Derby 119

Turkey Release 120
Hermit In The Woods 121
Hayrack Ride 121
Halloween Party 122
November 1St 122
Trail Ride 123
Thanksgiving 124
Deer Season 124
My Year Is Complete 127
The Creation Of Argyle Lake State Park 127
Argyle Lake State Park Dedication 1949 130
My Retirement 132

A Family Message 137
A Special Thank You 139
About the Author 141

DEDICATION

I dedicate this book to all who have enjoyed Argyle Lake State Park. The picnickers, fishermen, campers, boaters, cruisers, hikers and nature lovers, and most of all the children. The children who came on class trips and walked the nature trails with me. Many learned things about the woodlands that they might not ever have had the opportunity to see and learn. The children who enjoyed the playground and the animals. I have many fond memories.

PREFACE

I accepted the job of Park Ranger at Argyle Lake State Park in 1966. I had a very good job in the construction business, and even though changing jobs meant a reduction in pay, I found the idea of being near my family every day just too good to pass up. I feel that during my 25 years at Argyle I lived and worked the role of Park Ranger 24 hours a day 7 days a week. I gave it my all.

I loved watching the fruits of my labor improve the park and make it a wonderful place for all to share. Being an avid nature buff, it was a good choice for my wife Bette as well. We had 3 children to think about. Dennis had already gone off to the University of Illinois. JoAnne was a Senior in High School and Cheryl was an 8th grader. I felt that the timing was ok.

I stayed at the park until 1991. After completing 25 years at Argyle, I had such misgivings about retiring, but, when you have a job that consumes your life every day from morning until night, it can be quite taxing. I thought I would let the younger generation have the challenge.

I wanted to put my memories of this time in my life into print. Thinking that it might not be that exciting to the average person I put it on hold. After writing my first book IT WASN'T MY TIME, which was written about my WWII memories, I had so many people ask when I was going to write about Argyle, I decided at age 96 that I needed to get it done.

The title of the book, ARGYLE..A YEAR IN MY LIFE AS A PARK RANGER, allowed me to give a seasonal depiction of my job as Park Ranger as I remember it.. I describe many features of the park, and many times describe day by day happenings the way I remember. I wish I could remember all of those who made an impact. There were so many. I have named a few.

I've enjoyed reminiscing about my time at Argyle. I hope by reading my book it will spark a memory of yours.

Ranger White

Ranger Wayne White

INTRODUCTION

During the 60's and 70's it was a little different than now. We didn't have cell phones yet, not every house had a computer, our televisions did not have 200 channels. It seems to me that there were more outside activities.

In the winter there was sledding and snowmobiling.

In the spring people were beginning to get outside. They enjoyed walking the trails, watching for spring flowers, and getting boats ready for the summer.

Summer camping was a popular family summer activity. On Fridays when weekends began, campers were lined up at the registration building to sign in for the weekend.

There were often times when there was a waiting list to rent boats.

Western Illinois University was full. And full of kids that loved to party!

Fall was also a special time at Argyle. People were still camping, fishing, boating, hiking and having reunions. The Labor Day Celebration brought thousands of people to the park. The colored fall leaves were a breathtaking attraction.

WINTER

New Year's Day brought a new layer of fresh snow.

I knew for sure that there would be a lot of kids coming to the park to coast today. Having a lot of kid still in me, I decided to make their day a good one. It didn't appear to be extremely cold. But, cold enough that a bonfire would be welcome for the sled riders.

I had a half barrel that I had used before for a portable fire pit. I gathered some wood that was already cut and split for the shop furnace and loaded it onto a small trailer which I hooked up to my snowmobile with a rope. I drug it to the top of the hill near my house. I needed some cement blocks to set the barrel on to create a draft from below and also to keep the fire from being directly on top of the blacktop road.

Just before noon the first kids began to show up with their sleds, ready to spend a day of fun sled riding. It sure pleased them to find a fire already built for them.

After eating a sandwich for lunch, I decided to use the snowmobile to pull the sledders up the steep hill. After all sleds had arrived at the bottom of the hill, the first sled tied on to the back of the snowmobile followed by all of the rest. The snowmobile pulled at least twelve sleds up in a line. They all hung on until we arrived at the top of that steep hill. This went on all afternoon until it was almost dark and everyone left for home.

So much fun!

ARGYLE

SNOW STORM

The next Friday noon it began snowing heavily. I could tell that we were in for a heavy snow storm. It was about 3pm when I told the men working for me to put the paint away and take off for home, for if they waited until quitting time it might just be too late.

It snowed all that night and then began to blow and drift the 8 to 10 inches of snow. The entrance road to the park had 3 to 4 feet of snow drifted for at least a half a block.

A local neighbor, Van Edison, who owned a track loader, called me and asked if he could help. I told him that I thought that would be great, but I didn't have the contractual money to have him do the job. He said that he was sure that I would be able to make it up to him sometime later. He worked all morning with his big track loader and made it so we could get in and out. Since he was so near our maintenance building, we decided that he might as well park his loader in the heated maintenance building. He was glad to get his machine in for the night.

WINTER EMERGENCY

Early Saturday morning Ron Clark called to ask me for a favor. He was a friend and knew that I had a snowmobile. His cousin had brought a new baby home from the hospital and was about to run out of milk to feed the baby. He wondered if I would take some milk to them as their lane was drifted completely full and there was no way they could get out to go and get milk.

I told him that I sure would if I could get to the Colmar blacktop where their home was situated down a lane. I checked with the State Police and they told me that the east west roads were fine and I should be able to get to Colmar without any trouble. Ron came out and we loaded my snowmobile in the back of my pickup and took off with the milk. The main roads were ok, but when we got to his cousin's lane it became clear that they wouldn't be able to get out for some time. Ron had never ridden on a snowmobile before, so I gave him a very scary ride jumping snow drifts on the fly! He has never forgotten that ride.

SNOWMOBILES

When I returned home from doing my good deed, I received a call from some people from Rock Island asking if we had enough snow to go snowmobiling. They didn't get any snow in Rock Island and were looking for a place to play. I told them that we had received plenty of snow and our roads were closed around the lake so they would have 4 ½ miles that they could play on. Sure enough, in about 2 hours they all showed up with their snowmobiles on their trailers. I told them to "have at it". I soon decided to get my snowmobile out and join them. I met one guy by the boat dock and he told me that I was going the wrong way. I asked him who decided which way was right? All he said was, "those crazy son-of-a-bitches did". I turned around and headed right back for the shed.

One woman with their group ran her seadoo under a guardrail. The machine was torn up pretty bad, but she wasn't hurt.

My Brother-in-law and his wife came out to our house which was located in the park. His wife told me that she would like to go for a ride. I told her to get on behind me and hold on. We began riding through the west pines. I could hear the Rock Island group racing. We were just plugging along when all of a sudden one of them came right at us. They hit us with a slanting blow turning us up on our side. It didn't hurt my machine, but their Yamaha didn't fare so well. We were not injured but it was frightening for my passenger. The Rock Island riders rode until dark and then took off for home.

What a day!

CHRISTMAS TREE PICKUP

When the men showed up for work one morning after Christmas, I told them that this was the day we were to pick up Christmas trees in

Colchester. Colchester, Illinois is the town closest to Argyle. I figured two guys could handle this job, so I took one guy with me in the big dump truck and proceeded to pick up the trees. We finally got our truck full and had to return for a second trip. If we needed more, we could go to see Rueben Lavadiere who sold trees and had some left over.

On Tuesday morning, we wired cement blocks, which I had picked up from the block factory, to the groups of 6 or 7 trees and drug them onto the ice-covered lake with the old Ford tractor to perfect fishing places where they would sink upon the spring thaw. Under the water these trees created a positive habitat for smaller fish to get away from their predators, and as the plant tissue decomposed, algae formed for food and Mother Nature jumpstarted a whole new series of vegetation.

BOY SCOUTS CAMPOUT

A Boy Scout Master had some of his scouts at the park sledding. He asked if he could bring his troop out to the park to camp in the pines this weekend for their Annual Winter Campout. The pines seemed to be excellent protection from the wind. I approved a camping spot where they could have a big campfire. I suggested that they stop in the picnic area and pick up some portable fire places. Fire in the pine needles presented a fire hazard even in winter. Plenty of wood was provided for the scouts and all went well with the temperature. It was around 20°.

NOT ENOUGH PAINT

Winter was the time for maintenance. We hadn't done much work on the picnic tables that we brought into our work area last fall. I had been saving this job for the workers to do while I was gone to a meeting in Springfield the following week. I realized that there was not enough paint to do all of the tables. Maybe because I forgot to order enough. I called Bob Cashman, Ranger at the Nauvoo Park and asked him if he could loan us some paint. He said that he would drop some off on his way to the Springfield meeting. This worked out well and I repaid him his paint a month later. Now the men will have everything they need for the week.

RANGER MEETING IN SPRINGFIELD

On Monday morning, the weather was a bit warmer, and most of the snow had melted away. Bob arrived with the paint around 9am and we caravanned to Springfield to a meeting of State Park Rangers.

We had heard through the grapevine that this meeting would be anything but positive. Rumors had it that there would be no raises this year. We will see. I was a bit of a rabble-rouser at these events.

After we checked in at the hotel, we assembled in the ballroom for our meeting. All of the "big wheels" were there including the Conservation Department Director.

He began the meeting by breaking the news to us as gently as he could. No raises. He blamed the Illinois Congress for not appropriating enough money for raises. Just after he dropped the bomb on us, he left the meeting and was not seen again. He left the Superintendent of Parks to listen to the complaints from the Park Rangers. It seemed that we all had something to say. A lot of problems were discussed during the afternoon. It was nearing time for us to adjourn for the day. Many were thinking of "Happy Hour" and being able to drown their problems of the day.

Rabble-rouser Wayne had to say sorry fellows, but the meeting is not over until I get an answer. Public Health and EPA representatives were present at our meeting. I asked the Public Health Representative, "Did you cause all of us to have to put concrete pits under the outside toilets"? He replied that if the outhouse pit was not within 50 feet of the nearest well, his department was not involved. I turned to the EPA man, and he denied ever knowing of such an order. I said, "well I guess some Congressman must be in the concrete pit business... Let's Go to Happy Hour".

See you all at the poker game in room 410 at 9pm.

I did pretty well at the poker game but had to quit about 1am as you could cut the smoke in the room with a knife and my eyes were burning.

The next morning, we went at it again. The next thing on our agenda was to discuss law enforcement in our parks. The Department of Conservation had asked the State Police to help us. They said that they were understaffed and suggested that the Rangers be trained in law enforcement. The Department of Conservation had reached a deal with Southern Illinois University to train 6 Park Rangers in the next Law Enforcement classes. The decision was made to send the 6 Rangers with the biggest problems first. I was one of the six. Others chosen to go were the Rangers from, Starved Rock State Park, Chain of Lakes, Giant City, Morrison Rockwood, and one of our Regional Land Managers from Southern Illinois. This training would take place whenever they could work it into their schedule.

By the middle of the afternoon it had started snowing pretty heavily. It continued snowing all night and was still snowing the next morning. The decision was made to cut the remainder of the meeting short so we could all get on the road. Some had a lot further to go than me and Bob Cashman from Nauvoo.

About 11am we started for home. The roads were really bad. Bob was ahead of me behind a large feed truck. It appeared as though the snow was about 8 inches deep. We noticed a man with an endloader moving snow by the Bradford Elevator which was right outside of Springfield. We stopped and asked him to load our trucks with snow so we would have some weight for traction. I really don't think we would have made it home without that extra weight.

The trip home should have taken about 2 hours on a good day. It took us 4 hours to get to Argyle. Bob still had another 60 miles to go. I called him that evening to see if he made it ok.

The men had a lot of work ahead of them with the tables that needed paint and repair and I had a lot of mail to go through and phone calls to return.

I needed to call Springfield and let them know if I would agree to work the State Fair this year in August. I believe I will do this as it's a chance for me to get a break from the 24/7 routine at the park for a few days. As well as a chance for my wife, Bette, and I to do something together.

HELPING THE SHERIFF

While I was working on these things in my office, I received a call from the Sheriff, asking me if I could help him and the States Attorney verify that a certain person was camping here on a certain day two years ago. They had been told that this person of interest had been camping at Argyle. They needed to know if there was any way I could verify this. I was able to tell them that they were in luck because I had kept all of the camping permit receipts carbon copies. I spent an hour or two going through permits. Believe it or not I found the camping permit and was able to verify their person of interest's story.

The men had about half of the 150 tables fixed and painted. There are quite a few remaining.

CATASTROPHE AVERTED

On a trip across the dam I noticed that something had happened to the compressor on the tower that stands in the water near the dam. Ice had formed against the tower. This had caused the tower to break a few years back. The ice had frozen against the tower and thawed around the bank, When the wind blew over the remaining ice, it moved and caused the tower to break. I knew some of the people that had been involved in repairing this break. It had been no easy task as they had to build forms on both sides of the tower and pour cement while out in the water. This had stopped the leak but caused a terrible strain on the mechanism that opened the gate at the bottom of the tower. This gate was there to use if the lake was ever to be drained.

I told the men to get a boat and push it out to the tower as we didn't know how long the compressor had been off. Luckily all that had happened was a blown fuse, we replaced the fuse and since the ice wasn't too thick around the tower, we just broke it up with an ax. What a catastrophe this could have been if I hadn't noticed the problem when I did.

ICY HILLS

The weather forecast for the weekend was for very nice weather so I suspected that the college kids would have cabin fever and would be itching for a party. There was still ice on the roads going around the park. I had barricades up so people would not try to go around. Some of the hilly roads on the east side of the park never got the sunlight needed to melt the ice. Because it was so nice outside it was hard for people to realize that the roads were still covered with ice.

Sure enough someone thought that I had just forgotten to take down the barricades, so they moved them off to the side and drove around them. Well, part of the way. They got stuck between two hills and couldn't get out. Then came another visitor who saw that the barricades were moved and drove around them, ending up in the same predicament as the first car. The first person played the innocent victim. I really didn't care if he got out or not. However, I felt bad for the second one. But, I helped them out.

I took my wide tired tractor and a chain to get them out. I guess I should have known better because I ended up between the two hills with the other two cars! Thankfully, I had my portable radio with me. I called my wife, Bette, to call Ralph Bisby to come out with his wrecker and plenty of cable.

Ralph arrived and stayed on top of the hill to winch us out. There was just enough cable to do the job by adding my chain to the end of his cable. He finally got us all pulled out but by then it was nearly dark. When all of this was over, I put a sign on the barricade explaining why they were there. One more car did do the same thing. He said that I didn't need to help him. He was just going to leave his car there until the ice melted.

VACATION

Bette and I seldom ever took a vacation, but we had planned to take off a couple of weeks this year. My son-in-law's mother had a condominium on South Padre Island, Texas. It was always empty in February when she went to Mexico City where it was warmer. We were fortunate to be able to take advantage of a lovely place to stay while we were vacationing.

At the park, winter time was usually pretty routine. There were repairs to be made to picnic tables, signs, and boats. My men had been with me for years and knew what to do. My Assistant Ranger, Wade Moss, was quite capable of being in charge. He and his wife, Betty, would just stay in our house on weekends while we were gone. This way if there was a problem, he would be right there to deal with it.

We left for Texas on a Friday morning and made it to Marion, Illinois for the first night. A fellow traveler asked me if we liked to eat fish. He said if so, we should go down the street to Opal's Place for all the fish and shrimp you could eat. He was sure telling the truth. Some tables had shrimp shucks piled high in the middle of the tables. This was the beginning of many nights of getting our fill of shrimp on our vacation.

It took us two more days of driving before arriving at Padre Island. The home was beautiful. There was even a pool right outside of our front door. There was a nice restaurant within a couple of blocks. This worked out great. If Bette wanted to sleep in, I could walk and get her a doughnut. We had friends that lived in Brownsville every winter. Nearly every day we drove there to play dominos with them. If we were hungry for shrimp, we would just cross the bridge to Port Isabelle and go to Crazy Harry's Sea Food Shack.

Tomorrow we would start driving toward Illinois. All good things must come to an end. Maybe we will return next year. It was a long trip home. It was really good for us to get away for a bit.

We arrived back at the park on Friday evening. We just had to make a trip around the park. We found that everything was just as we had left it. It was nice to know that we could leave and not be worried about Argyle.

I called Wade and told him that we were home and he could have the weekend off.

CAMP GROUND HOSTS

People had been cooped up all winter and were wanting to camp.

Keith Solomon called me and asked if he and his wife, Vonna, could be Campground Hosts. I thought this was a wonderful idea. They were reliable and trustworthy, and I knew they would make good hosts. I told them to come on out and we would get them set up near the entrance to the campground. The Host Program was just great as it took a lot of pressure off of me making sure everyone was registered and paid up for camping. Keith and Vonna came out first thing the next morning and we picked out a camping spot that would be near the entrance to the campground. It just so happened that right after we got them all set up a camper arrived. They made out their first permit with no problem.

Concession Stand Before Remodeling

CONCESSIONERE

Our Concessionere, Wendell Haines, had a two-year contract. I wanted to give him all the help I could. He needed some tables and chairs. I got him a gas stove and some other things he needed last year at government surplus in Springfield. I called him and asked him if he would like to go down to Springfield with me in our big truck to get some things that were needed for the concession stand. He was very excited and pleased to have this opportunity for items at no cost. It was unbelievable how much was available at surplus. We were mainly looking for tables and chairs. We found some new ones that still had wrappers over the arms. I asked the man in charge why they would have brand new chairs. His response was that the General at the Armory had ordered new chairs and when they arrived he didn't like the color. And so, he sent them to surplus and ordered more. Our tax dollars at work. We got 6 tables and 24 chairs.

The truck was full when we took off for Argyle. Wendell was very happy. I told him that I would try and find a way to air condition the concession building. That made him even happier.

Remodeled Concession Stand

SPRING

The weather was getting better and better each day and the picnic tables were almost done. A couple of men started hauling them out to various spots around the park.

It was a nice weekend and we had about 30 campers for their first visit of the year.

Three or four pontoons are coming in each day.

Everyone is getting ready for summer!

SUMMER HELP

It was time to apply for our summer help. The powers in Springfield always wanted me to wait and hire college kids for our summer help. I wanted the help before college was out for the summer. Also, if I got older people, I wouldn't have to teach them every little thing and that would save time. We would only get so many man hours for the summer so I would ask to hire my first person from April 1st until October 1st. This took about half of my man hour allowance. I was only allowed 12 ½ for the year. I requested the second person to start May 1st, and the third to start June 1st. Usually they sent me a college student to start June 1st. Typically he would want to quit August 15th and that wasn't much of a problem.

The big parks (as the front office would call them) would always get a lot more help than little old Argyle over in "Forgottonia". So, I would get help wherever I could.

The government had started a Senior Program in which I was allotted 2 men 65 years or older for around 30 hours a week. These men were sometimes the best workers as they were more mature and knew how to work at most anything. All I had to do was post what I needed done and they did it.

During the summer months after school was out the State started the C.E.T.A. Program (Comprehensive Employment and Training Act) to hire some high school kids from lower income families to work for the summer for minimum wage. Each year I would get a different amount depending on how much money was budgeted for the program. They would mow, work on the docks, build trails, and paint. Over the years there were countless young men that worked for me at Argyle from our locality. I wish

I could name them all but I just don't have the memory needed. I really enjoyed these kids. This particular summer I was to get 6 boys over the age of 16. The C.E.T.A workers I hired for this year were: Kent Stoneking, Bob Woods, Richard Longcor, Jerry Hysel, Charles Fosdyck and Lanny Jones. They were a great bunch of kids that I really enjoyed working with. They weren't afraid of work, and I think I treated them pretty well. Every project we did we would make a game of it in some way. One day I had them working by the boat docks where we were moving concrete blocks. Jerry Hysel bet Bob Woods $1.00 that he couldn't carry 2 full cement blocks up a steep bank slope at the same time. Bob did it! Bob was a very stout young man. As it turned out, Jerry didn't have a dollar to pay his bet. The other boys made sure that Bob got his money on payday. Kent Stoneking was with me for a couple of years and I always had fun with him. He would always have something to say whenever they were given a job to do. One day I told them to get some sacks and pick up beer cans that had been thrown out in the pines. Kent came back with, "They will just throw them out there again". A couple of months later I had them do the same thing. I said to him, "Kent, you were right, they threw them out here again". These young men built most of the first trails that are still at the park. I always thought that the work that they did for me would help make them better citizens in their adult life. I hope that it did.

 There was another way I would get help that didn't cost the State anything. I went to the local Judges and told them that if they needed to slap the hands of a culprit in the courtroom, they could send them to me to do community service. Believe it or not I could sometimes get some pretty good help that way. One morning I got two fellows who were waiting for me to give them an assignment. They overheard me telling my men that we needed to cut the dead part out of a big oak tree. One of them spoke up and said, "I'll do it". As it turned out, these two fellows had been lumberjacks sometime before getting into trouble here. It was a treat to watch them trim that tree.

Wayne W. White

THE ZOO

Billy the Deer

There was a local lady, Janie Irish, who had a deer that had lost it's mother. She had raised it on a bottle. The little fawn never learned to fear people. She named the little fawn "Billy". As he got bigger, she decided to give him to me. The kids in the park loved him. He was always around while they played. Billy just ran loose.

Someone tied a red plastic ribbon on his horn. It was pulled way too tight. I was afraid that it would shut off the blood supply to his horn so I tried to get him to let me cut it off. He became leery and I finally had to wrestle him to the ground to get it off. It was too late. Just as I thought, the blood supply had been cut off and the horn died. After that he was a little afraid of me. Before I could put my arms around his neck, but no more.

Most of the people from the area knew Billy. He loved attention and that sometimes got him into trouble. Billy loved kids and sometimes he would go all the way into Colchester to the school where the kids all made over him.

When fall came along, I had a talk with Billy. I told him, "I don't know if you understand English or not Billy, but you must stay in the park because it is deer hunting season and I don't want you to be "deer meat". He didn't listen very well. He was going to town West of Mt. Auburn Cemetery and someone shot him. Some of the local people were all up in arms about it but there was nothing I could do. He was a deer and it was deer hunting season.

Bette Walking Billy Home to the Park

I decided to get some more animals and have a small zoo for the children. Some animals were in pens and some just ran at ease. The kids sure enjoyed feeding them. Our peacock brought a lot of attention, as well as the turkeys, ducks, chickens, and quails.

Larry Creasy worked for me. He had every kind of animal you could imagine. He brought over some rare breed of chickens and a turkey. I got a grouse from some people over by Bushnell. I went with Larry to Burlington to a swap meet of exotic birds and bought another chicken or two. I just kept them in makeshift pens I had made of chicken wire. The kids would hurry over from the campground every morning to feed the animals. I just loved watching the happy kids.

I had a couple of little foxes that we raised. My daughters named them "Charley Fox" and "Foxy Loxy". I had to keep them in a large pen behind my house so I could keep an eye on them. They grew up and climbed out of their pen and took off. They are wild animals and they needed the wild, but they were very young and hadn't been taught how to survive. At night after it got dark, I would shine a flashlight into the edge of the woods behind our house and sure enough their little eyes would shine in the dark. I would put out some food near where I would see them. In the morning the food would be gone. They finally got used to the wild and went on their way.

Charlie Fox and Foxy Loxy

One of our campers from Mundelein brought me a weasel for my animal zoo. This was a small animal that needed to be caged. I built a cage and put a hollow log inside for him to hide in. The people who gave him to me had captured him thinking they were trapping a rat. They weren't sure what it was when they brought it out to me. I kept the weasel for a couple of months until the zoo at Springfield found out that I had it. They wanted it to put in their zoo, so I decided to let them have this very rare species.

Bottle Feeding Baby Raccoon

LAKE ARGYLE'S PET CROW
Photo by Mavis
Campers and picnickers at Argyle Lake State Park who enjoyed the antics of the pet crow last summer may like to know that he is still having fun. During the holiday season he would pull off and hide ornaments from a decorated pine tree near Ranger White's house--where he only knew. He is free to go anyplace but he prefers to stay around people. He pays no attention to other crows that winter in the park. Ranger White thinks he doesn't know he is a crow.

We had a lot of pets at the park at different times. Many of the campers still remember "Jimmy the Crow". He would pick up acorns and drop them on the rooftop of campers. It made a loud noise and he got the attention he wanted. He was pretty ornery. I had Van Edison doing some work for me in the park. When the final drive went out of his tractor, we got it into the maintenance shed to work on it. Things were going well until Jimmy started taking the nuts and bolts and flew them up to the ceiling of the building and hid them in the I-beams. I know he thought it was funny that we couldn't reach them.

BECKY & AGNES

A couple of the bigger parks were given burrows to haul chips to the trails. This was a PR move by the Conservation Department that wasn't too successful. The Ranger at Starved Rock knew about my animal zoo and asked me if I would like to have Becky because he never used her anymore. I was pleased when he said he would even deliver her. When the Ranger from Rock Cut learned about the Starved Rock Ranger giving me Becky, he called me and asked me if I wanted Agnes. She was another burrow the State had bought. I didn't think they would be much trouble, so I accepted them. I had a local man make Agnes a harness so she could pull the sorghum press on Labor Day. I would usually just let them run loose around the Park. Everyone enjoyed them.

I had a friend south of Colchester named Genie Nelson. He had burrows and took Agnes for a visit to be bred. As luck would have it, Agnes had a "Baby Jack".

Burrows can breed in their own family. So after Jack grew up he became the father of "Baby Amos".

Agnes & Baby Jack

Grandsons Mike & Erik with Baby Jack

Wayne, Becky & Agnes

MILLIE THE PONY

It was my believe that at some point in every kid's life they wish they had a pony. I got a pony for my daughter Cheryl. She named her "Millie". I must say that Cheryl was sort of afraid of Millie. She wanted so badly to be able to ride her around. She tried and tried to ride her. Cheryl would get on Millie and Millie would take off running through the pines. We could hear Cheryl screaming "whoa". It was hysterical. We all loved Millie and Millie thought she was a member of the family. She would come up on the porch and try to come in the house. Bette planted tomato plants she would eat them. She would rub her face against the outside water faucet to turn the water on so she could get a drink.

On a warm weekend night there were lovers parked in the west pines. Their car was all steamed up. Millie approached the car and began licking the windows. I can't imagine what the couple in that car thought when that big tongue started licking the window. It scared the daylights out of them! They actually came and reported to me that there was a loose horse in the park. She was quite a pony.

EASTER

Every Easter morning the local churches held a Sunrise Service at the only shelter house in the park. I decided it would be the perfect place for a chapel. I had the materials I needed from the sawmill. I made pews from the slab of the logs with the flat side up to sit on. I sawed out planks for the stage and slabs for the podium.

The local churches went together and put on a touching Easter Sunrise Service at the Park. Argyle Church put up a lighted cross and tomb on the east side of the lake directly across from the Chapel on the west bank. This event brought large crowds of approximately 400 people. It was a very inspirational gathering. The tomb was lighted and when the sun came up, it came up just over the hill above the tomb. It was breathtaking.

Easter Sunrise

Wayne W. White

THE CHAPEL

This little chapel became very popular for a lot of outdoor weddings held there each year. I was very proud to offer this lovely area of worship to the public.

The Chapel

Wedding in the Chapel

SPRING FLORA

My wife Bette, was a true lover of nature. She was interested in all of the wild flowers at the Park. She documented where and when she identified plants. She knew the scientific names as well as the common ones. Her findings were acknowledged by WIU. She loved nothing better than to walk in the woods identifying, logging, and photographing rare species. I've included photos of the species she identified at the park.

Bette was also an avid birdwatcher. Again, she documented every time she spotted something new. We fed the birds in the winter. There were always many varieties of birds to see out our kitchen window.

Bette Birdwatching

Whenever she went into the woods our German Shepherd, "Pete", would go with her. One horrible day she thought she was having a heart attack in the woods. She had health problems and she knew she was in trouble, so she told Pete, "Go get Wayne"! I was way on the other side of the park across from the dam. Pete came running to me barking and wanting me to follow him. I knew he had been with Bette so I followed him right to her. I was able to get her to the help she needed. Thank heavens for Pete!

Pete the Dog

Bette spotted a pileated woodpecker several times. They are a very private bird and are not seen by many. She thought they looked prehistoric. We also welcomed an albino robin wwho returned 3 years in a row.

Pileated Woodpecker

MEMORIAL DAY WEEKEND

Memorial Day weekend was usually considered the beginning of the camping season. The year before we had been loaded with campers and I saw no reason that this year would be any different. Friday evening was pretty hectic. Two people would be signing in campers non-stop. We did not have numbered camp sites. We just let the campers jockey for the shade trees or other favorite spots. I observed some campers putting their rigs in intricate positions so that there would be room for their buddy campers to pull in so their awnings almost touched. If it should rain, they could go from camper to camper without getting wet.

I don't know how we got away without having more arguments over fireplaces and electric plug-ins. The campers did realize that our electricity was limited and they could not use too much or the fuses would blow. We would issue their permits and tell them to set up wherever they liked.

The Assistant Ranger, Wade Moss, and his wife were busy all day with permits. About 5pm, Bette and I went to the check-in station to help. It was a mad house.

We had a wagon loaded with firewood for campfires. This slowed up the lines a bit because campers would want to fill their trunks with firewood before moving on.

I went into town and got 4 big steaks and some potatoes for our supper. We put the potatoes in with the meat in aluminum foil. We cooked them right on the fire. While this cooking was going on the campers kept flooding in to camp. At about 9pm some campers with tents came back and asked if they could camp along the road. This was Memorial Day weekend and we allowed just about anything.

The flow of campers had slowed down now. At around 10pm a couple of older ladies pulled up and wanted to set up a tent. I told them that there wasn't much room in the park, but they could camp wherever they could find a place. Wade and Bette Moss went home, and Bette and I started our trip around the park to see where all of those campers that had come in had ended up. It was crazy every place. We had a good laugh when we finally arrived at home and found that those ladies had pitched their tent in our front yard! Oh well, that was okay with me.

We broke all records this year. When we filled out our camping receipt reports for Springfield, we reported 623 camping units for the week.

The camping season had officially started for the year.

TREE CUTTING

The first year that I was at Argyle it struck me that we had a very bad fire hazard as well as a disease problem with the pine trees being so close together. Pine trees that are starved for sunlight will only have dead limbs except for the top where they receive light.

I contacted Springfield and asked if we could harvest some of these trees to make our posts that we had been purchasing. The conservation person from Springfield that I talked to looked into it and found out that it would cost more to provide our own posts than to purchase them already treated. He investigated the hazardous conditions and was able to get me permission to cut every other row the first year and every other tree the second year.

In 1948 the foresters planted these trees every 4 feet. Nearly every one of them lived due to it being a wet year.

After cutting a few trees I just felt that we needed to use these logs for something. And then it dawned on me that we could build a log cabin. This cabin could show the public life in the olden days in this area.

THE WOOD CHIPPER

The Department of Conservation owned a woodchipper that was passed around to each park that needed it to chip up limbs. When it was our turn to get the chipper, we would make chips for the foot trails.

I was scheduled to get the woodchipper the next week. While we had the chipper, all workers concentrated on this job. There were plenty of trees to be cut on the east side. The men were cutting and trimming. The machine threw the chips into our big truck. As soon as the truck was full, we would dump the whole load at the beginning of a trail so the chips could be distributed at a later date after the chipper was gone. This was a good job for the high school kids that worked at Argyle during the summer.

I was going to do my best to get a log cabin built before Labor Day!

COLLEGE KIDS VS TOWNIES

I remember well one Macomb High School graduation party at the park. I had some trouble with a feud between the TKE (Tau Kappa Epsilon) fraternity and the Macomb High Bombers. If a TKE fraternity brother was to acquire a Macomb High Bomber jacket they collected a reward. If the jacket had blood on it the reward was much higher.

It was the same with the Macomb High Bombers. They were rewarded for getting a TKE jacket. A few evenings before this, a group of Macomb High students caught a boy and girl off the path in a secluded area. The students proceeded in beating the young man up. This boy and girl came to me for help. I was furious. I knew what had taken place and I decided that this had gone on long enough.

I planned a raid on their graduation night party. I had 2 county police, 2 state police, and the game warden helping me. These high school kids had learned the college kid's songs and seemed to know it all. And, of course, they had somehow acquired a keg of beer. They were whooping it up pretty good when the police and I arrived. There were two brothers that I knew that said to me, "It will take more than you to take us in". I replied, "I have help". With that they jumped in their car and started to drive wildly through the pines, only to pull up between two police cars. As soon as this group of kids realized what was happening, they scrambled in every direction. Another young man known well to me decided to climb up a pine tree. Trooper Spurlock was a part of the raid. He finally convinced this young man to come down out of the tree. When he hit the ground, he took off running. Spurlock never did catch him. I teased Spurlock about this for years later. One of the senior girls happened to be wearing short shorts. When she ran she got tangled up in multiflora rose bushes. Her legs were cut up pretty badly from the thorns. She was sitting in the back seat of the squad car with blood running into shoes from the deep scratches. We had never set out to hurt anyone; not even to arrest anyone. I wanted to make them understand that they were not going to get away with the antics that had been happening.

I wasn't trying to take sides against the high school kids, but I knew that the bomber kids would go to areas where the college kids had been partying, and after the well organized fraternity party had cleaned up their mess, the high school boys would dump the barrels of beer cups all over the ground trying to get them in trouble with me. It was actions like this that caused the graduation raid.

These young high school men turned out just fine.

THE GORDY TAYLOR STORY

Western Illinois University students used Argyle Lake State Park as a retreat. When I first became the Park Ranger the parties students had were mostly fraternities and sometimes their little sister sororities. I became really well acquainted with many of them. The Phi Sigs were my bad boys. It seemed they were always in trouble. My favorite fraternity was the Delta Sigs. Whenever they planned a party, their Advisor, Gordy Taylor, would always contact me to arrange a good spot for them to party. They knew the rules and tried to abide by them. In fact, Gordy would sometimes bring some fraternity brothers out to help clean up the park.

I distinctively remember one night when Gordy showed up at the park with a beautiful young coed on his arm. He told me that her name was Diana Paulson, and she was his blind date for the evening. Later in the summer I saw Gordy and he still had Diana on his arm. We remained friends over the years

After 50 years Diana is still on Gordy's arm. What a pair they turned out to be.

At my retirement celebration Gordy made a fantastic presentation in my honor. I'll never forget it.

Mr. & Mrs, Gordy Taylor

THE TERRIBLE STORM

It was late in April when a big storm hit. We had about 5 inches of rain in a very short time. That much rain pouring into the lake caused many problems. I had gone to the boat dock for my early morning coffee when I decided the coffee would have to wait because the boats that were chained to the docks were pulled so tight from the high water that the back ends were sticking up out of the water. I hurried up to the maintenance building to get some bolt cutters so that I could cut the chains holding them to the docks and let them settle to the level of the water.

Tommy Horrel had arrived at the boat docks to check on his dad's pontoon boat. He wanted to help. Wendell and Dottie Howe were camping in the campground and also wanted to help. The four of us managed to loosen the boats from the docks. Some of them did get away from us, but all they could do was float to the dam. It was difficult to get them away from the spillway because water was gushing over the spillway at about 2 foot deep. By noon most of the quick water from the flood had already gone over the dam to the creek below. By the end of the day we had all of the boats back in their docks.

I called the radio station and had them put it on the air that I was requesting all pontoon owners come out and rescue their boats. Most of them did show up and took care of putting new chains and locks on their own boats.

Spillway

SUMMER

Wayne W. White

THE BEAVERS

While on the lake in the patrol boat I noticed about a dozen trees on the bank of the lake had fallen into the water. After some investigation, I found that a family of beavers had chewed the trees off so that they would fall into the water. They eat the small twigs under the water after the lake has frozen over in the winter. After checking the area further, I discovered many more trees had been chewed down. This was going to ruin the tree line rapidly. I called Springfield and asked for permission to get rid of these destructive culprits. The officials at Springfield agreed that I needed to do something right away. Both of my sons-in-law agreed to help. After dark we went to the area where the beavers were working. One held a big light and the other a gun. There they were chewing down another tree. The gun went off with a bang. The beaver was dead. The rest of the beavers must have got the message because they did not come back to this bank. I knew I would have to keep a close eye on this problem.

THE COAL MINE

One day I was wondering to myself, "What did we have at Argyle that wasn't available at other state parks"? The thought that immediately came to mind was the coal mines that were strung up and down Argyle Hollow before the State of Illinois purchased the land to build Argyle Lake State Park. I could find where many of those mines had fallen in, but none that you could actually walk inside. I decided to reconstruct a mine entrance, just like one of the olden days. I realized that I could not go back into the bank allowing people to endanger themselves, but I could just build it far enough into the bank to show the coal vein as well as showing the hazards of the coal mining profession in a drift mine. The location I chose was easy to find a vein of coal without removing much dirt. I constructed a mine entrance that looked exactly the same as the real drift mines did in the olden days. I found a mannequin at a local clothing store that was being discarded for a newer model. The store owner gave it to me for the mine. I already had an old miner's lamp that the miners wore on their hats to see in the dark. Most miners used dogs or goats to pull carts loaded with coal out of the mine. At the entrance to the mine was a shack which held a potbellied stove. It was a place for the miners to come out of the mine about every hour to drink coffee and sharpen their picks. When they came out, they placed their picks in the hot coals. Within a few minutes the pick would get red hot, they could take a hammer a pound it out on an anvil to a sharper point. Back into the mine they would go for another load. In those days they spent about as much time shoring up the roof of their tunnel so there were no cave-ins than they did digging coal. It was a very dangerous occupation. Many coal miners did not go home after a day's work because they had been buried alive in a cave-in.

Information at the mine entrance explained that the first coal mine was created as early as 1850. The mines went far into the hills. They had rooms that branched out on both sides of the main track. Most mines were about 3 feet high.

Coal was extracted until the 1940s.

In the Argyle Lake area there was about a 25 inch vein of coal with a layer of clay about 10 inches thick below the coal. The miners would lay on their side and dig the clay out from under the coal vein so it would be easier to break the coal down having nothing under it. Some of the good miners could mine as much as 35 bushel of coal in a day. I believe that coal sold for about 9 cents a bushel at that time. The slack piles that you can see from the road between Colchester and Tennessee are from the clay that was taken from under the vein of coal. They had to get rid of the waste so they sent it to the surface to be disposed of. A few days after I got the mine entrance finished, a reporter came out from the local newspaper and took a picture and published a story about the mine.

About a month later, while I was at home eating dinner, a big black car drove into our driveway. On the door of the car it said: MINES AND MINERALS. The man driving the car had come from Springfield to inspect my mine! He had been to the courthouse in Macomb and he told me that at one time 31 mines were registered in Argyle Hollow alone. He just had to see mine. When I took him to the site, he was quite impressed that I had made such a great educational display. However, he did register my mine.

Coal Mine

DEATH IN THE CAMPGROUND

One evening my wife Bette and I had gone to Macomb to The Pizza Hut for dinner. Upon returning home we were met by County and State Police cars. These officers knew me and proceeded to tell me what was going on.

It seemed that a couple had rented a primitive camp site. When they arrived at their site, they found the charred body of a woman lying in the campfire! The campers immediately rushed back to the check-in station to notify the camp ground host. Together they called law enforcement. The dead woman was recognized by one of the officers. Her husband had been camping with her. The officers ordered him to be picked up.

There had been a murder in the park!

This was way more excitement than we were used to. I hurried up and changed back into my uniform and headed for the crime scene.

There was already a man there from the Illinois Bureau of Investigation taking pictures of the body. The body was that of a young woman approximately 21 years old. Her clothes had been pulled up over her head and set on fire. The fire hadn't burned the way whoever set it had planned. The fire had burnt her shoulder and the side of her face. The sheriff told me that her husband was a suspect. The Colchester Fire Department brought out a portable generator to light up the area for investigation. The man from the I.B.I. (Illinois Bureau of Investigation) had seen enough and had the body taken to the morgue.

The next day I reported this incident to Springfield. Since the I.B.I. was involved they didn't need to be involved.

Argyle Lake made the headlines for a few days.

PICNICS AND REUNIONS

Argyle Lake State Park was a popular place to have reunions and picnics for many people. Some of the largest reunions were the Hornbaker's, the Creasey's, the Wayland's, and many others including the VFW once a year, which drew large crowds.

Every Sunday morning you would see someone sitting on a picnic table reserving the spot for their family to attend later.

photo courtesy of Janet Sowers

photo courtesy of Janet Sowers

photo courtesy of Janet Sowers

FISHING

Our fishing was pretty good for a long while until there was overcrowding by smaller fish. People would tell me that there were no fish in the lake. But the problem was that there were too many fish causing a stunting of their growth. When a fish gets stunted growth, it won't bite because it's stomach has shrunk and it doesn't need food. A fish is a glutton as long as it has the correct environment. When overpopulation occurs, the problems begin. Predator fish are needed to keep the young fish from growing up. It takes quite a balancing act to create the right balance between bass and bluegill or crappie. Fish biologists wanted to draw the water level down as part of their management program to balance the fish population. The boat owners were all against this. Most of them just used the lake for recreation and not fishing.

The boat owners demanded a hearing about the water draw down. A meeting was arranged on a Wednesday evening at 5pm so the fish biologist could explain his plan. The boat owners showed up in great numbers. Representative Clarence Neff was present along with newly elected Senator Laura Donahue.

Mr. Kenny Russell, the fish biologist, began to explain how the draw down of the lake would help the fish population. He was heckled at every breath. After about 20 minutes of Mr. Russell struggling to speak the representative stood up and told Mr. Russell that he would have to find another way to manage the fish. That brought a roar from the crowd. The meeting abruptly adjourned.

Grandson Jason's Fish

(Future Fishing Guide)

LITTLE FISHERMAN

I was at the boat dock and overheard a young boy asking his dad to rent a boat and take him fishing. The father apparently did not want to go fishing. He was growling and gripping. When his wife got involved, he reluctantly rented the boat and purchased a small pole, line, and worms. After a lot of arguing, they began rowing out of the boat dock area. The little boy threw his line in the water. Immediately a huge catfish took the bait! It was a whopper. That was one happy child. It did my heart good since the dad had thrown such a fit not wanting to take his son fishing. It made my day.

Stites Family

Jack Stites, our local pharmacist, had a boat tied up at the boat dock and enjoyed the lake very much along with his family. His son, Tom Stites, told me that their family spent many days here at the park having picnics and fishing.

RELEASE FISH—Kim Russell (left), state fish biologist, and Wayne White (right), Argyle State Park ranger, released 1,302 fingerling channel catfish Monday in Argyle Lake. The fingerlings had been fed in a holding basin at the park since last May during which time they doubled in length from 3 inches to 6½ inches. The reason for using the holding pond system is because of the increased costs for small fish. Plans are being made to repeat the procedure next year.

Fish Release

PONTOONS

When I became the Ranger at the Park there were 13 pontoon boats docked at the lake. Springfield thought that was too many and encouraged me to get rid of them. They ordered winter removal of the pontoons which I believed that they hoped would discourage their return in the spring. They wanted the lake to be strictly for fishing and not recreational boating.

Most of the pontoons at that time were homemade. They were barrels with a deck built on top of them. Some were built with closed in cabins on them with all the luxuries of home built in. Many cookouts took place on pontoons out on the lake. There were no mosquitos out in the middle of the lake. That made cook-outs quite pleasurable.

Swimming was not allowed in our state lakes. People would put about 6 pontoon boats in a circle so no one from the outside could see the swimming going on in the middle. I knew what was happening but I honestly felt like they did... why not.

Before I retired from the park our pontoon enrollment had increased from 13 to 43. The state still stuck by their guns and made us remove them in the fall. With so many pontoons we had to build more docking space. It cost the pontoon owners $50.00 per year to leave their boats tied up for the boating season so the concessionere took in a lot more money. It was very inexpensive recreation for many outdoor enthusiasts.

It seemed that everyone wanted a pontoon. If you happened to have one for sale it was quickly purchased by a new owner. It seemed that new owners spent a lot of time on their boat the first year. A little less time the second year, and by the end of the 4th year it had a For Sale sign hanging on it. Soon it would have a new owner and the fun would begin all over again.

Wayne W. White

HELP FROM THE GAME WARDENS

The Conservation Department had asked the State Police Department to give the State Parks some weekend help. The State Police rejected the request because they were short-handed. Until there could be law enforcement training for rangers, the Conservation Department decided to have the State Game Wardens come to the State Parks on weekend evenings to provide whatever help they could.

This Saturday night I was to get help from two game wardens from within the State for the first time. I knew they were in the park somewhere. I needed to talk with them, but I was unable to find them.

There was a college party going on that I stopped to check on. I noticed that one of the college girls was wearing a Illinois Department of Conservation hat. I just knew that my game wardens had to be in this group of kids somewhere. Sure enough, there they were dancing in a group of college girls. Good help.

GYPSIES

The Gypsies

Every year we had some of our Romanian friends come to camp. They were commonly addressed as gypsies. That is how they referred to themselves and what they wished to be called. They usually had between 4 and 29 campers and lots of trucks. The King would take care of the camping fees and I would deal with only that one person. While I was at the park there were only three families left that were active; the Mitchell's, the John's, and the Ortiga's. The Mitchell's were the largest of these families.

While they were camping at Argyle, the King became very ill. They took him to Chicago and there he passed away. That meant that his wife, the Queen, was now the ruler of the family. All dealings and transactions had to be done only with her. I remember this one particular visit they asked me where they could get some chickens. I told them if they would walk down the hill just outside the park, they would find Williams Produce. The next day after they left the park, I spent a great deal of my time cleaning up feathers!

While they were camping, they would go into Colchester to the local grocery store for supplies. They visited Denney's Grocery Store. Quite a few of them went into the store at the same time. A few of them got into an intentional argument at the front of the store causing quite a ruckus. The manager went to settle the dispute leaving his office and a half-opened vault unattended. While John Denney was settling their problem, the rest of them cleaned out his vault! They were known for this kind of antics. Some people were afraid of them, but I had no problem.

After the King passed away, and they were camping, I told Mrs. Mitchell that the park was for camping and her boys could not work out of the park. That was agreed upon. They were known for going out and contracting to paint a farmer's tin roof or something like that using inferior paint. Just after signing them in to camp, I called the local sheriff to alert him that they were in the area again. The sheriff called me the next day informing me that he had a couple of the boys in jail. He wanted me to have their Queen come and bail them out. They had robbed someone and the robbery had been reported. I went to the campsite and found the Queen. I explained to her that the boys were in jail and that I would take her to go and get them. She seemed very surprised, but happy that I would do this for her. After she had paid the victim back all of the money the boys had taken, the sheriff let them go with the understanding that they were not to come back. On the way back to the park, the Queen said, "I guess this means that we will have to leave". I reminded her of the agreement she made and that they would have to go.

The next year the John's came to camp and we had no trouble. They had a wedding in the campground with the brightest garments I'd ever seen. They only stayed a couple of days. I could have bought a nice CrisCraft boat from them for a song, but I was pretty sure it was hot so I didn't bite. I think this clan as I knew them are now extinct.

HOT AIR BALLOON RIDE

For my wife's birthday I decided to get her a hot air balloon ride.

I contacted Terry Argenbright from Blandinsville and made the arrangements for him to come to the park. Bette was very excited. We went up in his balloon on August 26th. It was quiet up in the air (except when the burners were firing). There's a feeling of motionless while moving. Most of all the beauty of the bird's eye view was breathtaking. We both loved it.

I decided to buy a balloon ride for my camp ground hosts, Keith and Vonna Soloman, for all they had done during the summer as hosts. They did a splendid job and helped me more than I could say.

Wayne W. White

IRON AXMEN

It was a very hot weekend and a lot of campers stayed home due to the heat. A motorcycle group called "The Iron Axmen" showed up to camp. These men had camped here before without a bit of trouble. The biggest guy in the group was named George. I told him the rules for motorcycle groups camping and he assured me that we would have no trouble at all. Everything went well. Many of these men were lawyers and businessmen. The majority were employed at Caterpillar.

AQUA CLOWNS

A few young men in Colchester decided that they wanted to form a local Jaycee organization. They wanted this organization to do good things for their city as well as help the poor and disabled. I remember a few members. Larry Sears was their President. John Churchill, Tom Dorethy, Charlie Mullens, Kay Beckerdite, were members. During this first year of their existence they were in the park more than once. They were collecting trash and cans. They decided that they would become better known in the area if they were to support a big event at Argyle. They approached me about having a water show with Aqua Clowns performing on the lake. They had contacted a group from Quincy, Illinois that provided water shows. They had selected a Saturday just two weeks away. This wasn't going to give me much time to get a permit from the state. My request did get approved 10 days before the show. The program was all set to go. The local media picked it up and did a good job advertising the show. There was a lot of excitement about the upcoming event.

The fish biologist read about this event and immediately contacted the state to get it stopped.

The time was growing closer so the answer to the objection to the water show had to be coming soon. In fact, it was getting so close that the fisheries got in touch with their law enforcement division and asked them to come to Argyle during the event and arrest me for allowing the lake to be used for something other than fishing.

My Regional Land Manager heard of the upcoming arrest and quickly went to a higher echelon of the State Department of Conservation and made them realize that my standing with the public was very good and if they did what they had planned it would be costly at the ballot box. The big wheels called off the threatened arrest and the show was on. The Colchester Jaycees did a fantastic job. Thousands of people enjoyed the lake that day and believe it or not it didn't hurt the fish one bit.

After a successful afternoon when more people enjoyed the lake than ever before the newly formed Jaycees had planned a fireworks display for after dark. I allowed them to pull some floating docks to the middle of the lake. The display could be seen from all directions. Everything went well and the Jaycees first big event was a huge success.

DIVER TRAINING

One Monday morning while I was working on the weekend camping report, a WIU professor and a couple of his students came into my office to ask if they could use Argyle Lake as a training place for divers. One of these students was Jerry Lewis from Good Hope. I thought for a while and decided why not. I stipulated that every diver be accompanied by another diver, and that they would not be conducting these training sessions on weekends. Everything was agreed upon. In later years I did use these divers for various recoveries.

POLITICAL MANEUVERS

When I took over the reins at Argyle, it seemed that I got just about everything I asked for. Things had been let go for a while because of the previous Ranger, Dale Lewis's health. We needed water in the newest campground, and our roads were quickly deteriorating. I requested a well driller to drill a well in the campground first. This was when I was introduced to the world of politics. I knew a well driller from Colchester who had drilled a well in the park previously. I found out that because he voted on the wrong political ticket, he would not be chosen to drill during this administration. A well driller that was of the same political persuasion as the current governor showed up to drill the well. I had no problem with this, but it did open my eyes as to what I could expect in this job. I soon learned to play the game.

When I was told that I could have a regular employee, I would have to contact the County Chairman of the party that was currently in power for the name of someone that he wanted to get a job. This was the way things were done in state politics, so I had to go along to get along. I fought this procedure throughout my entire tenure at the park, but the system was bigger than me.

Another example of political maneuvering was when we were given the order to install concrete pits under all of our outdoor toilets, even if they were located in the timber. I had to comply with this order although I resisted as hard as I could. I had used wooden pits with cracks in the sides so liquids could seep out and fertilize the trees. You could throw a little lime in the pit and there was no odor at all. When we installed the concrete pits the liquid did not escape. It was terrible! You just could not control the smell anymore. As I mentioned earlier, I brought this up in a Ranger meeting in Springfield. The public health representative in attendance on the panel of discussion along with another man from the EPA knew nothing of these orders. It had to have been another political maneuver.

At a meeting just after the governorship had just changed to a different party, our supervisor addressed the meeting of park rangers, "we are going to change the color of our picnic tables from green to Pittsburg Rustic Bark Brown". Me being the rabel rouser in the meetings, I said, "Does this mean I have to use Pittsburg White"? That brought a roar from the crowd. They all understood what I was getting at. White is white no matter what the brand. The Pittsburgh Paint Company must have kicked into the campaign fund pretty heavily to get a deal like this. Changing paint for all the state parks is A LOT of paint.

SILTING OF THE LAKE

Silting

When the lake was built and it filled with water, the engineers and surveyors estimated that there would be 117 acres of water surface when the lake was full. This I presumed to be true. A survey of water surface in 1968 disclosed that there was only 93 acres of surface water because of silt. I went to Springfield to inform them that the lake was filling in with silt at an alarming pace. A man at the front office said to me, "A lake is only good for 109 years". I thought this was such a stupid remark because silting can be stopped if the watershed is secured. A watershed of 4000 acres would be quite an undertaking. If we could just own enough of this watershed to get vegetation started on it, erosion could be stopped somewhat, or it surely would help. After a lot of debating with the powers in Springfield I was finally able to convince them that we should try and purchase another 1000 acres and I would try to correct the problem. Now that I had someone believing that I was right, I had the task of getting the Land Acquisitions Department to come up with enough money to buy the land. With budgets being so tight, my request was tabled for about 4 years. When the purchase became possible, the acquisition department thought that we should buy the most vulnerable land first. There was about 180 acres that drained into the boat dock area. That was an area that I just had to have to keep the dock area from silting full. I knew which land was needed the most. I also knew that this property was going to be the most difficult to purchase. It was owned by a local auctioneer named Huey Martin. It was definitely going to be difficult. It certainly was difficult as we finally had to get the land condemned so we could use the Eminent Domain Law. The state sent a purchasing agent to join me in a meeting at the Martin house. The purchasing agent that was with me had enough authority to make an agreement that day. Mr. Martin had tried to sell this land to his tenant and I knew the dollar amount. We offered him far more than that amount, but to no avail. He said to us, "I know how much this land is worth, I sell more land than anyone in the United States". We realized that we were going to have to condemn the land to purchase it. Proceedings were started to use the right of eminent domain. After 4 months, court proceedings were started to condemn the land. Huey Martin would sometimes ship cattle in from Texas and feed them on this land that we were trying to purchase. The cattle would cause the land to get stirred up on the surface, and when it rained all of the loose dirt would come right into the boat dock area. At the court proceedings the first thing our attorney asked Mr. Martin was, "you feed a lot of cattle on this land don't you, as many as 50 head"? Mr. Martin boastingly replied, "oh no, more like 1000 head". That was the worst thing he could have said. The Judge knew that 1000 head would stir up more soil than 50. The ruling went our way, but when the court set the price it was based on the appraisal price from appraisers that Mr. Martin had hired. The Judge set the price of the land much higher than it was worth. It was unbelievable but Mr. Martin decided that it still was not enough. He took the case to a higher court in Canton. He passed away on his way to Canton to testify. I have always thought that he could have afforded to donate the land and have his name in lights on it. Maybe his death would have been prevented by not having the pressure of trying to get more money out of the state. By the time we got through all of these court proceedings the money that had been allocated had been used up somewhere else in the state. We had to get in line again! It took another 3 years before we were allocated the money. We did, however, finally get the land. We had no problem with the other purchases.

The second parcel of land contained the Adkinson Cemetery.

THE ADKINSON CEMETERY

It was a Monday morning and I was in my office working on weekend camping reports. A couple came in to talk to me. The man was Virgil Foster, a local genealogist, and the woman was his friend, Goldie McCord. They asked me if I knew anything about the Adkinson Cemetery that was located on the east side of the park. After a bit of conversation, I learned that Goldie was the granddaughter of John McCord who was buried in the cemetery.

I knew about this old forgotten cemetery. When I first came to the Park in 1966, I decided to find it. After searching for a long time, I came across the Adkinson Cemetery. Trees had grown up and pushed the stones over. A lot of the state's famous multiflora roses had spread to the area as well. You could hardly walk through the area. I thought it might be an attraction for park visitors to see. I used a weed mower and made a path to the spot. Without my path it would be nearly impossible to find this area. The state had not purchased this land, but when I convinced the department of land acquisitions to buy our watershed, this land was included in the purchase. I was on the lookout for some iron fence that was sometimes used in old cemeteries. I wanted to make this another park attraction. One day a man from the Conservation Department was at the park for another reason and I told him about the discovery of this cemetery. He wanted to go and see it for himself. I instructed him how to get there. When he returned, he said that he had thought about stealing the gravestone of a slave. I absolutely did not want anything like that to ever happen. I decided that I would just let the brush take over my path. At least until there was a way to control the area.

This cemetery had a history that told of the controversy that John McCord faced because he insisted on having his man slave buried with him in a white man's cemetery. I agreed to take Virgil and Goldie to the cemetery. There was no way they could find it on their own.

I was interested in this history as well. They followed me to the east side of the park where we began our walk. They were so excited that they had found someone to show them the abandoned cemetery. Virgil Foster was excited to do research on the families buried there. Goldie told me that her grandfather John McCord had shocked the community by insisting that his man slave Jack be buried in the white cemetery. He stood his ground and "JACK THE BLACK" was interned in this cemetery.

Virgil, Goldie, and I spent 3 days obtaining information. Virgil and Goldie walked around examining headstones documenting the list of families. I uncovered buried stones, cleaned them so they could be read, and checked dates. Sometimes I would find many family members near each other. If the dates were within months of each other, we wondered if their deaths could have been from disease such as cholera or smallpox. When I found a young woman's head stone I could sometimes look nearby and find a small infant. So many young women died during childbirth in olden days. Included with those buried there was William Willard, a Revolutionary War Veteran.

After the work was finished, I went to the McDonough County Historical Society and talked with them about our findings. They were delighted with this new information.

John Fentem, who lived near the entrance to the park, told George Jones, our local undertaker, about the Adkinson Cemetery. George was interested in cemeteries and especially this one due to the fact that there was a black slave buried in a white man's cemetery. This is a photo of John Fentem and George Jones with "Jack's" gravestone.

John Fentem & George Jones

MISSING BOY

It was a Saturday morning and a bunch of children were playing together on the playground. A mother walked up and asked the kids where her son was. One little boy said, "he must have drowned cause he's not here". This mother just went crazy. She came running to me crying. She desperately needed help. I called the Colchester Fire Department and asked them for help searching for this lost little boy. It seemed that we had everyone in the park searching. After at least an hour of searching, someone drove across the dam by the spillway and there was the little boy playing in the sand by the creek. It was such a relief. No one knew how he got that far away. What a horrible scare.

CAMPERS

A big rain sometimes meant campers need to be pulled out onto the blacktop. I really didn't mind, and it would prevent big ruts in the ground.

I went down to the boat dock and everyone was wearing raincoats. Their spirits may have been dampened a bit but not enough to make them give up a weekend day that had already been planned as a fishing day. Some were renting boats and others were buying bait. They told me, if it rains before 7 it will quit before 11. That old saying usually works.

I told the campground host that I would run a few toilets (check them out for messes or need for toilet paper) and then I would get the wide tired tractor to pull campers out as they were getting ready to leave. When I checked the toilets, I found a couple that were really bad. I was sure that whoever dirtied them up did it on purpose. They had crapped in the middle of the floor instead of the stool. I was glad that I had taken a bucket of water with me because I really needed It!

When I got back from cleaning toilets, the rain had let up. Most of the campers decided to sit it out until afternoon. I fed the animals and then told my wife, Bette, that I was done for the day unless something else came up.

Wayne W. White

WIU THEATRE PROGRAM

Instructors of the WIU theater program came to me and asked about the possibility of presenting some student written plays for the park visitors to enjoy. I thought this would be great for Argyle. I hoped that I would be able to keep the area quiet so the actors could perform uninterrupted as they did not have microphones. These plays were written about the Civil War in our area.

We decided to experiment with the plays on Thursday evenings. This might be the best evening for me to be able to control the noise.

Each Thursday evening we would pull the bleachers to the west pine area. It was a great place for visitors to enjoy the plays. Bob Kazlowski, Director of the Conservation Department, loved the idea. In fact, he wrote the first play. It was a huge success, so we put these plays on for most of the summer.

THE WINDMILL

One day my Land Manager came to Argyle for a visit. He saw the windmill that I was keeping for posterity. He asked if he could have it for the Big River Park in Gladstone, Illinois, to pump water for the horses. They had a lot of trail rides at that State Park. They have sandy soil that has a water table less than 15 feet from the top. The windmill would help them. I agreed to give my windmill to Doss Henshaw, the Ranger at Big River. He was really excited to get it. He had a flatbed trailer that could haul it and was ready to come over whenever I wanted. I had the legs in cement so I just took a cutting torch and cut the legs off at the ground. I let him know when I was ready. He came to Argyle and we loaded it with my end loader and it was on its way to Big River.

SQUIRREL HUNTERS

Some squirrel hunters showed up to hunt in our public hunting ground. Our Conservative Department was always quick to brag about the hunting area that we provided but failed to tell the public about all of the restrictions there were. Squirrel hunting was legal in our zone starting August 15th. However, we could not allow hunting in the park until September 15th due to safety reasons. There were still quite a few visitors walking the trials within the hunting area. I happened to personally own some land near the park. I offered to let them hunt there. It seemed to satisfy the hunters to hunt on my land instead of in the parks. If I hadn't had a place for them to go, they would not have been very happy.

RAINY SUNDAY

This particular rainy Sunday, I got to watch Meet the Press on TV. Something I hadn't got to do since the previous spring. I loved that show. It felt good to spend a lot of the day with my wife. She prayed for rain every day.

I checked the pines area out just before noon and found a couple of groups that had decided to stick it out in the rain. Each group had a small shelter to put their food under, but most of the tables to eat on were out in the rain. Most of them started pulling out just after they had eaten lunch. I only had to pull out one camper. He could have probably made it but I always suggested that I help.

At about 3 o'clock Bette and I got in the truck and went for a ride to check out the roads and some of the boundary signs. I had been told to get more signs around our circumference. I did realize after our ride that I needed a lot more signs. When we got back in the park, I took Bette to see the progress on the log cabin construction. She was surprised that we weren't further along considering how long the work had been going on.

The next day I got the student workers busy on stripping the logs so we could get them finished before the park enrollment increased in the middle of August.

Everyone left the park and we had a quiet evening.

Some campers had invited us to come and eat hamburgers with them. We usually didn't do this as it would possibly cause problems between campers. With almost everyone gone we accepted. We had a good time visiting with our friends in the campground. I decided to skip my 10pm trip around the park due to the rainy weather.

LOCAL BIKERS

It was Saturday evening and I was at the registration booth signing in campers when a large group of motorcycles from Warsaw, Illinois arrived and wanted to camp. There wasn't any problem with this. I would have them camp in the west pines a long way from our family campers. I picked out the biggest guy in the group and appointed him as the group spokesman. I gave instructions that they were not to ride around the park after 10pm. They didn't seem to mind this rule.

It wasn't an hour later when another large group of bikers from Abingdon arrived on their Harleys. I remembered that these two groups had had trouble in Nauvoo the year before. I explained to them that I knew about the trouble in Nauvoo State Park with the group from Warsaw. I told them that the group from Warsaw was camping in the west pines and if they were to camp, they would have to camp in the same area. I announced to all of them that if there was any trouble between them, I would have every State Trooper in the state here and they would have to pay the consequences. They got along fabulously. They explained to me that the problem that they had gotten into in Nauvoo was over a stupid patch on a leather jacket.

The evening went very well but I had not laid out the rules for the next morning. Sure enough the next morning at 5am they all cranked up their bikes to ride around the park!

One of the groups had a van that some of their friends rode in. It broke down right in the big campground. This didn't set very well with the trailer campers, but most were understanding and knew that it was just one of those things that happens.

It was Monday morning August 4th. The sun shining in my bedroom window woke me up before 6am. A new day had dawned and there were things that needed to be done and I did want to put as much emphasis on the log cabin as I could. Two of my regular employees went to haul logs and all of the summer help kids went to strip logs. We didn't do any building yet as I wanted to take advantage of the summer help kids while I had them. My permanent crew could finish building the cabin even if it took all fall. Things were going pretty well until one of the kids cut his hand on the draw knife that he was using. He had his own car, so I let him drive into town to the doctor to see if he needed any stitches. The doctor just cleaned it up, applied a bandage, and sent him back to work. I put him on a push mower for the rest of the day so he wouldn't get his hand dirty. We worked all day at these jobs and made a lot of headway. The kids that were stripping pine logs all day got really sticky. I felt that if I could get in 3 or 4 more days of stripping like this, we would have enough logs for the cabin.

The Log Cabin

After the men left for the day, I asked Bette if she would like to go out on our pontoon and fish a little bit and maybe cook some hamburgers. She said it sounded good to her. She called our daughter JoAnne and her husband John to see if they wanted to go out with us. They said they would be out in less than an hour. I had time to round up the hamburgers, buns and bait. We got started about 6pm. On the way out onto the lake, my son-in-law lit the charcoal so it would be ready to cook in about an hour.

The boaters out on the lakefront didn't realize that they might see

Ranger White on a pontoon boat instead of his patrol boat. I did catch some swimmers. All I did was make them get out and promise not to do it again. Of course, promises are made to be broken. It was also a good chance to check for preservers. I would always say, "everyone grab a preserver". If there was anyone left without a preserver, they would have to go into the concession stand and rent one or get off the boat. They usually went the rental route as they weren't about to leave the beer source.

We were ready to eat about 7pm. Bette began catching some pretty good bluegill and did not want to stop and eat. We spent the next 2 hours just fishing and visiting.

When we got into the dock about 9 it was already pretty dark. There were pontoons still out on the lake. They were probably waiting to see if the coast was clear to swim again. At 10pm I made my nightly rounds. Everything was ok. There were still 2 pontoons on the lake. I flashed my lights at them. I am sure they knew what that meant. It was 11 before I got them in to the docks and gone.

SCARE WHILE MOVING PONTOON

One of the pontoon owners had a couple of barrels leaking under his boat. He pulled his pontoon up on the bank to replace the bad barrels. After his repairs were completed, he asked me if I could help him get his pontoon back in the water. I went to the shop and got the tractor with the end loader to push the boat back in the water. The first push almost did the trick, but the last barrel got hung up on the bank. I got off the tractor to help push it in by hand. But.... I forgot to set the tractor brake! As we pushed the boat the tractor began to move forward. I tried to jump back on the tractor but stumbled and fell down. The tractor was rolling, and I was rolling into the water. The rear wheel of the tractor stopped on top of my foot in the water! Most of my body except for my head was under water. I couldn't move. The people across the lake at the concession stand as well as my wife had watched it happen. Bette quickly called a local man, Ralph Bisby, to come out immediately, bring his wrecker, and pull the tractor off of me. I wasn't aware that anyone had observed what had happened. It was so hard to keep my head up. I was thinking of having someone cut a hose on the tractor so I could breathe underwater. My foot hurt so bad. I just knew it was crushed. I still wasn't aware that help was coming. There was a lot of commotion all around. People were running around and panicking. In my head I was panicking more than anyone. Then finally Ralph Bisby arrived and pulled the tractor off of me. Whew... that was so scary. My wife took me to the hospital to get an x-ray of my foot. The x-ray showed that my foot had survived with no broken bones. The water and the soft mud had cushioned my foot. I guess it wasn't my time.

The next morning it was a bit cloudy. The weatherman didn't act like we would get much rain, if any. My wife of course wanted rain, but I had work in mind, so I prayed for no rain. We did have a little shower about 10am but it didn't amount to much. I was kind of taking it easy with a sore foot. It was a good thing that it was cloudy, or the humidity would have been unbearable. There was a flat tire on the wagon that we used to haul logs. That slowed the crew down for about 2 hours. Things went well the rest of the day. When it was time to quit the sun came out.

Next week I was to work at the State Fair in Springfield so the crew should get the logs done during that time.

When nighttime came, I had the same issue as the night before. A couple of pontooners thought they had the right to stay as long as they wanted since they rented a pontoon space. Sometimes they would purchase a camping permit and stay all night on their boats. That was ok with me. I just wanted to make sure everyone was treated the same. Some of the pontooners did cause some trouble for me but that just goes with the job.

A VISIT FROM TROOPER HOCKER

One night before I made my 10 o'clock ride around the park a friend of mine, State Trooper Bob Hocker, paid me a visit. He had heard my many stories about running drunks out of the park at 10pm, and wanted to see firsthand how I did it all by myself. He got in with me and the first group we came to was in the east pines. When we told them it was 10 o'clock and time to put the fire out and leave. They began to open their cans and pour the beer onto the fire. Bob was amazed that there was no argument. He told them that they might as well open two at a time because they were going to have to empty them all. It almost brought those kids to tears as the poured the last can on the fire.

Trooper Hocker found out firsthand what I deal with. I told him he was welcome any time.

It was Tuesday morning. I woke up this morning and headed for the boat dock for breakfast. I usually didn't eat too much, but this morning I had ham and eggs. I sat and ate breakfast with some fishermen from Pekin. Their fishing trip had been successful, so they decided to stay an extra day.

As soon as I got into the office the phone rang. It was just a reminder about my working obligation at the State Fair next week. I would be staying at the lodge on the south end of Springfield. Most of the motels were booked up because of the fair.

When the men came to work, I decided that they had better work on fixing a footbridge that we had been putting off. I wanted to get some other things done so they would have plenty of cabin work time while I was at the fair. The two senior workers got on the riding mowers and hooked onto a small trailer that we used to haul small trimming mowers and weed eaters. This pulled two of my C.E.T.A workers off the logging job. They were glad to get away from that sticky pine sap.

About 8:30 a young couple came into the office to ask about using the Chapel for a wedding next week. Most weddings had been in the spring so there were no conflicts. I explained to them that if they were going to have a party with beer at their reception, they would have to go to the picnic area. They had already made plans for their reception in town.

They had just left when the game biologist came in to discuss the hunting regulations for next year. We both decided that we couldn't change the start date because there were too many people in the park. We discussed releasing some turkeys the next spring. There were already a few in the southwest end of the county, but none here in the park. He wanted to enlarge the hunting area, but I convinced him that we had better leave well enough alone. He had brought forms with him for us to fill out on the squirrel /rabbit count for when the season started. He also brought more hunting signs. We really needed the extra signs.

As soon as he left, I went to check on the bridge repairs and the mowing crew. I told the men working on the bridge that they could go to town and pick up more 2 x 10's to make sure the bridge was fixed correctly.

Usually in August the grass doesn't grow much, but there were always a few places that need trimmed up. It was hard to make it look as good as it did in the spring,

At lunch time I was approached by the county dive team. They wanted to stage a drowning for training purposes. I told them that it would be ok if they did it on a weekday. They were hoping for the next Tuesday.

After lunch the men went back to their jobs and I went to the Division of Tourism office to ask for help advertising our special event on Labor Day weekend. The woman in charge of the tourism assured me that they would pay for some ads in the local papers as well as help getting the word out at events that they would be attending.

I went to the courthouse and found out that one of the people that I had arrested and was to appear the next day had pled guilty and paid his fine. I will still have to come in tomorrow for another case.

On the way home I came upon a woman and her children along the highway with a flat tire. I didn't believe she could have ever gotten it changed by herself if I hadn't come along. She didn't have a Jack. I got the tire fixed and got her on her way.

By the time I got back to the park it was nearly quitting time. I just waited for the crews to come in and report their progress. The mowing crew needed another full day, the bridge crew should be done by noon.

I had a pretty good evening. All pontoons were in by 10 and not many lovers around the park. I watched a little of Johnny Carson's The Tonight Show and went to bed.

Wayne W. White

WIZARD OF PLAY

Grandson Christian

The Wizard of Play

Combining Yankee ingenuity with a childlike sense of wonder, Wayne White created a playground like no other

By Dave Ambrose
Public Information

ON WARM SUMMER weekends at Argyle Lake State Park, Colchester, an eclectic collection of slides, swings, tunnels and trolleys swarms with kids while other, more traditional playgrounds languish in picnic areas nearby.

There's a structure with a ramp, a slide, a firefighters' pole and a swinging bridge that would give Indiana Jones second thoughts. There's cargo netting to climb, a covered fire escape to slide down, a glider to ride, and (if you have the chutzpah to jump off the tower) a hand trolley to ride down a 50-foot length of cable. It's a playground to end all playgrounds, a creation that looks as if Rube Goldberg, PeeWee Herman and Frank Lloyd Wright's son — the guy that made Lincoln Logs — got together to play one afternoon.

But this playground is no collaborative effort. It emerged, piecemeal over the last six to eight years, from the imagination of Argyle Lake Site Superintendent Wayne White.

At 68, White's slightly elfin appearance betrays his ability to intuitively know what children think about and come up with one-of-a-kind, inexpensive playground equipment to unleash their imaginations.

Two axioms guide White's efforts: 1.) Kids want playground equipment that is challenging, both physically and mentally, and 2.) Kids like to climb.

"I remember when I was a kid, I liked to climb," White said. "I've always known that kids like heights. They'll crawl up in a tree just to be getting up high."

He glanced around, looking for an example to illustrate what he was saying. It didn't take long. A pre-teen girl approached an elevated playhouse, looked around and casually clambored up the ladder.

"Look at this girl here," said White. "She's a big girl, and there's no reason for her to climb up there. She just wanted to get up where it's high — that's all."

About eight years ago, White launched the playground with a simple structure incorporating a ramp, slide, firefighters' pole and swinging bridge. Since then, he has been expanding on the play area with at least one new piece of equipment annually. This year, it was a tunnel under the combination slide tower and trolley platform that dominates the area.

The inspiration for the hand trolleys was a mid-summer experience with White's 8-year-old grandson. To amuse the youngster, White stretched a downward sloping rope between two trees in the back yard of the site superintendent's residence, a few yards from the playground. An antique hay pulley was threaded onto the rope and a burlap sack suspended from the pulley served as a makeshift seat.

"I talked him into climbing up there and jumping on that sack. He was scared to death, but Grandpa told him to, so he did it," White recalled. "He loved it! Down he'd go, you know, over to the other tree. And I got to thinking, 'Why wouldn't that make good playground equipment for kids to play on?'"

White's enthusiastic speech about playgrounds and play equipment often is peppered with such self-directed musings.

White built the frame from 6- by 6-inch lumber milled from white pines that had been thinned from the park's plantation. He modified the design of his trolley so users had to hang on to a trapeze-like handle.

"I got to thinking that if they sat on that, they could put their fingers up into the pulleys," White said. "So I had to keep their hands busy."

The trolleys immediately proved popular among the playground set. White said he looked out one day and saw 21 children waiting in line for a chance to slide down the rope.

"My 6 by 6s were starting to bow because I had so much pull in one direction," White recalls. "So I said, 'Wait a minute. Why don't I make that two ways. Then I'll only have 10 kids waiting in line, and I'll have pull in both directions so it won't bend my 6 by 6s.'"

Wayne W. White

LOG CABIN

I wanted to get more done on the log cabin while I still had C.E.T.A workers. We were getting up high enough now with the logs that it was hard to reach with the endloader. Just before noon a log rolled over the top of the bucket and broke a hydraulic hose. Luckily the log stopped behind the bucket and did not come down on the driver! I went into town and got another hose while the men ate their lunch. I got back at 12:30 with the hose. We didn't lose much time at all. We made 2 hooks that would fit on the bucket. This would allow us to go up 2 more courses. It was time for the men to go home before we finished. One of the C.E.T.A workers asked if he could work his last day on Friday instead of tomorrow. That was a good deal for me. I would have him mow the park entrance before the weekend.

WIU DORM REUNION

I was getting ready to leave the office when a young man about 25 years old came in to see me. He was planning a reunion of his dorm to be held Saturday and Sunday. Some of the former students were from the

Chicago area and all points west. I knew this would probably be a drinking bunch, but I was hoping they would be a little drier behind the ears. They were older and were probably married. He told me he expected about 15 families. I began thinking of where I would put them.

SPEAKING ENGAGEMENTS

I was to speak to the DAR (Daughters of the American Revolution) this evening, so I needed to go and get cleaned up. I wasn't sure what I would talk about. I usually gave a brief history of myself and then explained the history of Argyle Lake State Park. I never had any problems speaking to groups of people. I arrived at their meeting at 6pm, and was treated like royalty. After the roast beef dinner, the ladies had their business meeting. Then it was my turn to speak. They were a good group. They seemed more interested in my military service than the park. They told me that they enjoyed my talk and informed me that I could be a member of their organization, as my Great Great Grandfather served as a soldier in the Revolutionary War. When I got home from these speaking engagements my wife, Bette, would always ask me how it went. I would always reply, "piece of cake".

Bette and I made our 10pm trip around the park. We found one college drinking party. Summer school was ending, and they were probably having their last hoorah. Most of them decided that they wanted to stay all night so I sold them a camping permit. I made it a group permit. It was the same price and a lot less writing for me.

LAST DAY FOR C.E.T.A. WORKERS

The morning sun was shining hot. At 8am it was already very warm. While I was at breakfast, I picked up some ice to put in the men's drinking water. Today's work would be in the shade. That would help. When the workers arrived to work, we started right in on the log cabin. The only stripping to do were poles for the rafters. This went pretty fast. At noon I told the C.E.T.A workers they could go home as soon as the rafters were done. This was their last day. They seemed really happy. They hurried to finish their job and by 3pm we were thanking them for their service. I surprised the men and told them to go on home too, it was just too hot. The men were much appreciative.

I knew there would be some swimming in the lake. It would be a temptation if I were in their shoes. I didn't think I needed to police all of the time. After all, I was supposed to have help from the game warden this time of year. I just went in the house and plunked myself down in front of the air conditioner. At about 6pm, I suggested that we go to town and have dinner in a nice airconditioned restaurant. She thought that was a good idea.

We didn't get back until 8pm. We stopped at the campground and talked to Keith and Vonna, our campground hosts. There wasn't much traffic, so I doubted there was activity going on over on the other side of the park. No trip around the park tonight. I watched the news on TV and went to bed.

The next morning was another scorcher. We were able to get another course done on the log cabin. It took all day as this last course had to be level so the rafters would line up correctly. I was so happy when the last log was in place. It had been quite a project. I felt that it was well worth the time spent. We quit a bit early again because of the intense heat. The men decided that they would rather come in early tomorrow to avoid the late afternoon heat. I visited a couple of campgrounds and there was not a soul in sight.

Everyone was in their campers by the air conditioning. I decided I might as well do the same. My wife wanted to stay home. There was a pizza in the freezer that we would eat for supper. By 8:30 it had cooled down enough to go for a ride around the park. I didn't really expect to see anyone, but it would be a change of scenery. When we got to the boat dock area, I could see some pontoons were out on the water. There was no doubt in my mind what they were doing with it being so hot. At least there was a group of people so they could look after each other.

It was Friday now and when I woke up there were clouds in the sky. That would hold down some of the heat but if it should come a little shower and the sun comes out the humidity would be terrific. The men were coming in at 7 because of the heat. I told them that we should get the entrance mowed before it got too hot. We had many other things that needed to be done. We had spent so much time on the cabin that some other things had been put off. They had the entrance mowed by break time. After break they took the weed mowers and started working the foot trails. That was a shaded job. I drove the old truck halfway around the park and left it there for them to drive back in at lunchtime.

The first family of the dorm floor party arrived and wanted to know where they were going to be setting up. I told them that they could put their trailers in the campground, but they would have to party in the picnic area. I was sure that this group would not want to quiet down at 10 like the other campers. I told the campground hosts to try and save around six spaces near the first one so they could all be together. Some of these campers had little kids but that didn't stop them from remembering the good old days at the park.

Daughter Cheryl on a Foot Bridge

The men finished the second half of the foot trails a little before quitting time. I sent one man to put sand under the playground equipment and the others to feed the animals.

Being Friday night there are a few campers coming in for the weekend.

I hoped they would camp where the electricity was good enough to run their air conditioners. Many of the camp sites had too small of wire and fuses to run very many air conditioners at once.

The problems began at about 6:30. The breaker released on the first campsite. I moved one of their cords to another circuit. That took care of the problem…..for now.

My wife called me on my radio and asked me what time she should put my hamburger on the grill. I told her to go ahead and cook. The evening cooled down nicely and I really enjoyed the hobo dinners she made. She put two hamburgers with sliced potatoes in between them with carrots and onions. They were wrapped in foil and then just put on the charcoal. It took about 40 minutes to cook. They sure were good. After dinner my wife and I sat at the camper registration booth with the hosts until it was time for my 10 o'clock rounds. When we got back there was another family of the college reunion pulling in. They had driven down from Chicago after work. We took them to a spot right next to their friends that had come from Decatur.

I told the hosts that they could go to their camper and go to bed. My wife and I would stay up awhile to see if there were going to be anymore campers. I did turn around some lovers that were not planning to camp.

When I got up this Saturday morning, I wondered what the day would bring. The park was in good shape for the weekend.

On my trip around the park this morning, I saw that the fence on the dam was loose on one end and needed to be fastened back into place. Also, some of the bolts had come out of the floating docks. These are jobs that the men could do while I was gone to the courthouse to defend a ticket I had written to a lad for driving in an unauthorized area. He had cut some terrible ruts and finally got stuck. When I found him, I told him that I would get him out, but I would also be writing him a citation. He seemed pleased with this outcome. He would plead guilty. I must appear anyway.

The men came in and asked me to get a tractor tire fixed while I was in the city. They loaded it into the truck and I was on my way. I had to appear at 10am, so I didn't have much time. I dropped the tire off at the tire shop and hurried to the courthouse. When I got there the Circuit Clerk told me that the young man had pled guilty and paid his fine. I decided to pick up a few things at the hardware store while I was in town. It would be nice to buy things as we needed them but the powers in the state capitol didn't want us to have a petty cash fund so we could actually save some money.

I got back to the park just before noon to find some people waiting for me. One was a college student wanting to interview me for one of his class projects. I was getting so I knew all of the questions as I did so many of these interviews each year. I always tried to spend some time with them, asking about their future plans and try to give them advice about job opportunities.

The state public relations officer was here and we planned to have lunch. He brought his wife with him, so I got my wife and headed for the restaurant in town. I had known this man and his wife for years and there wasn't another person from the state that I would have rather worked with. After lunch we made a tape about the year's events at the park. We talked about our summer plays, our hunting programs, and of course our big Labor Day celebration. The Labor Day celebration brought many thousands of people into the park. We also talked about my homemade playground equipment and how it is always busy. I showed him additions that had been made to the park since he was here last.

After he left, I checked with the men. They hadn't had any problems with the fence or the floating docks, but they ended up replacing quite a few rotten boards. I took Wade Moss, my assistant, and showed him an area where jeeps and 4-wheel drive vehicles had been coming into the park. I told him that if they had time next week, while I would be working at the fair, they could put some posts up to stop this encroachment. When we got back to the shop the men were just getting ready to go home.

A beer truck pulled in and wanted to know where the group was that ordered the beer. I knew it was the graduates that were having a reunion of sorts. I decided to take the delivery man to the campground where they were camping so I could lay down the rules before the keg was tapped. I reminded them that I had already made a deal that this party would be held over in the picnic area and not in the campground. That was all right with them. They took off for the picnic area as soon as the beer truck left.

I was sure glad that I was able to catch this party before it got off on the wrong foot.

I checked the animals to see if they had food and water and then went to the storage barn to get a couple of bales of hay so there would be plenty for next week. While I was getting the hay, I saw a horse trailer at the horse campground. They hadn't registered to stay all night. I went back later to see if they planned to stay. Some were reluctant to pay if they were not prompted to.

RUGBY

When I got back with the hay a couple of college boys were waiting for me to get permission to have a rugby tournament this year in our west field. We had an ideal place where they could play 3 or 4 games at a time. They could play an entire tournament in one day. I approved with the stipulation that there would not be any alcoholic beverages involved. They agreed to anything to get the field. Everyone knew that there would be beer but maybe we could hold it down a bit.

As soon as they left, I checked with Bette to see what she wanted to do for the evening. I didn't foresee anything that the campground host couldn't handle. She suggested that we go out to eat and take in a movie (for the second time this year) and I agreed. As soon as I got changed, we stopped and told the campground host where we would be and took off for Macomb. The dinner was good and so was the movie.

We returned to the park just before 10pm. We decided to make the rounds in the car before we retired. Everything was pretty good. Usually there were no problems when the college was not in session. I finally went to bed at 11pm. I needed to rest up for a big weekend. Quite a few reunions were planned, and I needed to be ready.

BASS TOURNAMENT

When I got up, I hurried to the boat dock for my wake-me-up coffee and prepare for the day. When I got there, I saw about a dozen boats lined up at the boat ramp ready to launch their boats for a bass tournament. It was a chilly morning. I saw that they had charcoal burners in their boats to warm their hands. Fishing would start at 7am and end at 11am. When the weighing took place, the fish were to be alive. After weighing they would be released. Next weekend they would be going to another park.

This was a good attraction for our park. These tournaments didn't take up much of my time. Sometimes there was congestion around the loading ramp, but it would never last long.

The next day when the men got to work, we planned out their day plus the next week. The mowing had to be done, the garbage had to be taken care of, and the animals had to be fed. We were to have a very large company picnic on Saturday. While the men moved picnic tables, I checked the playground equipment to make sure that everything was safe for the hard weekend use. I found a spring broken on the trampoline and more sand was needed under the rope trolley. I got one of the men to help me and we replaced the spring and put the protective net in place. After the tables were moved, they all jumped on mowers and went to work on beautifying the entrance. Also, the ball diamond needed to be dragged. These picnics always have a big game as well as volleyball and horseshoes.

SWIMMERS AT THE DOCKS

At noon I went and got Bette, and we went to the boat dock to have a sandwich. After lunch we started to leave. A group of young people had decided to take a swim right there by the boat slips in front of everyone. I felt that some citations needed to be issued. When I told the two that were in the water that they would have to come up with the bail bond, they both said that they didn't have any money. A boy on the bank said that he would take care of it. He pulled out a roll of bills that would choke a cow! I filled out the tickets and took the two swimmers to the post office to mail the bail bond and tickets. I kept thinking about where that boy could have gotten that huge roll of money. I tried to dismiss my thoughts of drugs. Who was I to know the answers.

About 2:30 I saw some kids racing around the lake. I stopped them and found that the driver was a 16 year old with a 14 year old passenger. The car belonged to the 14 year old's father who was an automobile dealer. I called the father and explained the problem. He did not seem one bit upset with his son. I guessed it was his business now.

At about 4pm. I drove by the picnic area to see how the beer party was progressing. All was ok.

Evening came and again I went to check on the party. It was now 10pm. I told them to keep the noise down. I didn't want drunks going back into the campground raising hell all night. They were well behaved. I had no complaints the next morning.

Also, on this 10pm run, I found some lovers. I asked them to leave. I really felt kind of bad because they really were not hurting anything.

I called it a day at 11:30.

On Sunday, August 17th, there was to be a fishing tournament. I didn't have to get involved in that as they all know the rules.

CHILD LEFT BEHIND

Sunday early evening most of the campers had gone home. I was standing at the playground watching some children play. Bette came running out of the house to tell me that a woman from Peoria had called and upon arriving home from a camping trip to Argyle had discovered that her 8 year old son had been left behind! We frantically began talking to the kids who were playing on the equipment. Sure enough we found their son playing among all of the children. Bette and I discussed what we should say to the little boy. We decided to tell him to keep playing at the playground and his parents would be here in a couple of hours to pick him up. We would keep an eye on him. Those parents must have been terrified.

HORSESHOE TOURNAMENT

There was also going to be a big horseshoe tournament. After lunch I went over to the horseshoe courts and was introduced to the state champion horseshoe pitcher and some others that were as good as the champion. I watched the play for a while and then decided I was a little out of their league. I invited them to come and use our park for their tournaments anytime. They informed me that we would need 2 more courts to be sanctioned. I promised that would be done soon.

I was called to the boat ramp area where there had been a fender bender. One of the cars was a corvette. The fender just broke like glass. I called the state police to come and fill out the accident report. When the trooper arrived, he took over the accident situation.

I spent most of the afternoon watching the kids on the playground. After about 3 hours I could see why kids get hurt. They will try anything. Nothing is too daring. I knew that there needed to be a challenge involved for kids to stay attentive. I would continue to think about this.

When evening came, people began to leave the park.

The sanitary dumping station plugged up. I was able to get it repaired so the campers could get on their way home. Only the campers who were staying a week or two were left.

WORKING AT THE STATE FAIR

Conservation World

My wife and I loaded the car and left for Springfield to work at the fair. I went on duty the first day at 3pm. We went directly to the fairgrounds. I worked a 4 hour shift and then went to our hotel room. My wife went to the exhibition area and looked at quilts and other wonderful things while I worked.

I stayed busy for most of my shifts. I wrote fishing licenses and answered questions about new laws that would be coming out. My wife came back at 8:30. There was no business, so I left and we went to the hotel. After we checked into our room we decided to go for pie and coffee. We went to the hotel cafeteria and ran into others I knew that were working the fair. We slept in late the next morning. My shift didn't start until 2pm. We decided to go shopping for a little while and then went to the amphitheater and watched some sheep dogs at work. We got a snack at a church stand before I went on duty. There was a bingo game next to the snack tent, so Bette decided she would just play bingo all afternoon. I got off work at 8pm and we went back to the hotel for some TV.

We slept in again the next day which was such a rarity for me. My shift started at 2pm so we decided to take in some more of the fair. It seemed like a vacation. Bette decided she wanted to see a stage show. Willie Nelson was the artist. We got her a ticket and then went to Conservation World to see what was going on. We rode the sky lift back to the concession area. We had a brat and it was then time for me to go to work. Bette played a little bingo and then went to watch some groups entertain. She came by my stand before going to see Willie Nelson. We made arrangements as to where we would meet when the show was over. I was really busy, so the time went quickly. When the next crew came to take over, I talked one of them into trading shifts with me for in the morning so I could go home instead of staying another day.

The next morning Bette got us packed while I showered. We went to the hotel cafeteria and had breakfast. Bette decided to sit in the entertainment tent and listen to the different groups play and sing. We ate lunch in the church tent. I could hardly wait until my shift was over at 2. When that time finally arrived, we didn't tarry. We got on the road for a good trip home.

It was just after 4 o'clock when we arrived home at the park. I had just missed the men. We went over to see how much progress was made on the log cabin. Not much really but other things could have come up. I checked in with the campground host and got a report of the week. Not much had happened. I checked in with Wendell, the Concessionere, and he had a good report also. Then I checked on the animals. Sure enough they had food and water. It had all been done.

We went into town to visit our daughter JoAnne and her family to give them a report of our trip to the fair. We went back to the park, went through the mail and glanced through the piled up newspapers.

We decided that we could go away more often and everything would be ok.

After my morning tour I was very pleased that everything I suggested the men do while I was gone was complete.

Monday morning was here. The summer was just about over. The C.E.T.A workers were done for the year. Only a short time until the college is back in session. We needed to start getting ready for our special event that is held at the park over the Labor Day weekend.

The men started hauling logs over to the sawmill area for the Labor Day show. Some of the logs from the log cabin that were not useable because of being too large or cracked, would be sawed into 2 by 10s for extra floor joists, and sheeting for the roof and floor. The log cabin will have a floor as most cabins had at about 1910. It would take about a week to get enough logs hauled in to keep the mill running throughout the celebration. The fellows that ran the sawmill really liked the pine logs as they sawed easily and provided a good show for the public to watch.

DRY LEAVES CAUSE FIRE

It was now Tuesday morning and still no rain. It was getting pretty dry and I worried every time I saw a fire somewhere in the park. Then it happened. A car had run off the road and his wheel went in a hole. I tried to get him out for so long that the leaves under the car near the muffler caught fire. Then the fire started into the woods. It didn't hurt the car too badly, but it did cause a problem when the fire started down the hill. I ran and got the men from their jobs, grabbed the backpack fire extinguishers and rakes and headed for the fire. We fought this fire until 4:30. It was time for the men to go home. I went around and reminded all of the campers to be extra careful with their fires.

Wednesday morning the weatherman said that we might get some rain. Sure enough, it rained and it rained hard. The oil needed to be changed in the trucks and tractors. The blades on the mowers were getting dull. There was enough work to keep everyone busy inside while it rained.

On Thursday we received a big truck load of supplies that I had ordered from the state. The men unloaded the truck. I did the evening routine as usual with my wife by my side. It never seemed like such a long day if she was with me.

On Friday I took a ride around the park and found that a large tree had fallen near the road. I had 3 men take the truck and chain saws to cut up the tree. I had them cut the wood up small enough that we could use them in the shop furnace in the winter.

The entrance was nicely mown for the weekend.

Someone had backed into the pay box at the equestrian campground. Two of the men took the tractor and went to straighten up the box. They also fixed a broken hinge on the gate. I took the ton truck and went to the rock quarry and got a load of gravel for one of the parking lots. We spread the gravel and then the men were done for the weekend.

I checked with the campground host to see how much camping money he had for me to deposit and to make sure he had plenty of camping books. He had about $400.00, so I made out a deposit slip and headed for the bank. While I was in town, I decided to order a pizza for me and Bette and the campground hosts. It was Friday night so the campers were pouring in. We ate the pizza in between camping registrations and visited all evening. This would be the last weekend the hosts would handle the campers on Friday and Saturday nights as I would be scheduling my assistant, Wade Moss, to work when the college was in session.

A couple of times I had to go down to the boat dock to rent a boat. Wendell had closed at 8 o'clock and these campers wanted to fish all night.

Wayne W. White

Assistant Ranger Wade Moss

LABOR DAY

The next two weeks of preparation for Labor Day celebration were a very busy two weeks. Monday morning when the men came to work, we sat down and discussed what had to be done and when it had to be done. We knew we had to pull some posts, rearrange some bumper blocks, get some logs to the saw mill, and get the sorghum press ready. I sent one of the men with an electric checker to see how many fuses needed to be replaced. This was something that could be done and forgot about early. I took the other two men and showed them which posts to pull and reminded them as soon as they got them pulled that they needed to fill the holes with sand. That meant they would have to go to town and get a couple tons of sand. We didn't need that much so we used the rest of the sand under the playground pits. This kept those two men busy for most of the day. When I checked with the men moving bumper blocks, they had put them where they would be in the way of another vendor so we decided we would just take them completely out of the area so they wouldn't be in anybody's way. While we were discussing where they should put the blocks the man checking the electric outlets came and said most of the fuses had been stolen and he would need quite a few. I had him to stay and help with the bumper blocks while I slipped into the hardware store to get a good supply of fuses. I was sure I would be needing a lot of fuses during the busy weekend. As soon as I got back with the fuses, I decided I had better check to see if we had enough logs near the saw mill. I wanted to be sure we ended up with enough sheeting for the roof of the cabin and also some for the floor that we planned to put in this cabin.

By noon the men were done moving bumper blocks with the end loader. I had them take a few more logs to the sawmill because there would not have been be another time to get them. The other crew spread the sand under the swings and then they went to the old sawmill pile of sawdust and took some of it to an area where we could get to it easily in case it rained over the busy weekend. The fellow had all the fuses replaced so I took him with me to start laying out spaces for craft people. Most of them needed about 30 feet, so we made sure there was enough space to get them all in. We had to take in to consideration where the 30 by 180 ft. tent would go for other craft people who needed to be under a shelter. We marked the spaces with white spray paint so we could find them easily. With this project partly done we ran out of time so we continued it the next day. When we got to the shop the mowers had come in and I was well pleased with what they had accomplished.

The next day there was 30% chance for rain. After breakfast, it began to rain. We did some things in the shop until the rain quit. This was a good time to take one of the trucks to the state garage in Monmouth, if we could get in. When I called, they told me to bring the truck in and they would get right on it. They usually wanted us to leave our equipment and come back another day to pick it up. We all thought they just wanted one of our state park trucks there so they could charge their coffee time to our trucks instead of the DOT trucks. When the men came to work, they drew straws to see who had to take the truck to the garage. Boone liked to go there and sit and watch those guys waste time. One of the seniors lost the draw so we sent him on his way. We had a table outside of the shop that needed a new board and a riding mower that needed an oil change and blades sharpened. This kept them busy until the rain stopped.

RUGBY TOURNAMENT

Two boys came into the shop to ask if they could have a rugby tournament in our park again as they hadn't made much progress in talking the college officials into letting them have it on campus. I told them they could play here and I would mow them a field but they needed to have their after tournament/ beerfest someplace else because last time the drinking had gotten a little out of hand. This they promised to do. The Rugby Tournament was to take place this coming Saturday so that wouldn't affect our Labor Day celebration.

CUTTING WHEAT

The Saturday before Labor Day, some of the Gas Engine Club members got together to cut the wheat that we had planted so that it would be ready to thresh during the Labor Day festivities. Paul Powell had to be there because he was the only one who knew how to thread the binder twine through the binder. I thought I knew how to put a nice load on the hayrack. I had lost my touch as half of my load fell off.

I had forgotten that this was a big week for campers to come in to get set up in a favorite spot before Labor Day and I hadn't checked with the host about the money he had taken in. I decided that I had better take him a couple more books and collect the money he had taken in so I could get it to the bank. He had over $500 hidden under his mattress. He told me the registration of campers hadn't let up a minute even in the rain. The rain finally let up and we were allowed to get back to the things we had to do to get ready for Labor Day.

The animals were out of hay, so I sent one of the men in my pickup to move a bale of hay into our barn. We would continue working in the shop until after lunch. I took the money to the bank and picked up a few extra singles for change.

When I returned from the bank there was a fellow there from the Gas Engine Club asking if there was anything he could do to help get ready for our big event. I gave him 2 bundles of laths and told him if he would number them from 1 to 130 that would help. He even volunteered to sharpen the ends so they would easily drive into the ground.

After lunch I told one of the men that was familiar with the sorghum press to go and cut a crooked tree limb that would work for the sorghum press. It had to have a pretty good crook in it so that the end would be low enough to attach the harness onto the burrow that was going to pull the press. The pole would have to be at least 25 feet long. He took one of the seniors and went on a search.

The phone in the office rang and it was a flea marketer from Missouri wanting to set up here on Labor Day. I told him we were full for this year, but I would put his name on the list to get an application for next year. He wasn't really satisfied but it helped when I told him to call the Lions Club in town in Colchester and see if they had any openings. Colchester was also going to be packed with vendors and flea marketers. I would be getting a lot of calls like this one.

We had to get some old wood for the fire pit under the sorghum pan. After the sawmill began running they would get slabs from there to burn. I told them there were some boards left over by the barn where we had torn out a picket fence that I felt would get them by for a while.

Our truck rolled in from Monmouth with some signs that I had ordered. We unloaded them before the men left for the day. Tomorrow we would get back at it again.

LABOR DAY VENDORS

An estimated 70,000 visitors attended our Labor Day celebrations. This was a wonderful opportunity for flea marketers. There was a flea marketer from Texas that traveled the country setting up at different shows all over the country all summer long that said Argyle was the best of all.

In past years it seemed that each vendor wanted to be the first one here. They would race through the pines looking for their name. A friend who worked for the auxiliary police, helped me change the assignment system to numbers instead of names. If they didn't know their numbers until they arrived this would eliminate the confusion.

NATURALIST HIRED

Since Argyle Lake had been recognized as a major state park, I was authorized to place a Naturalist on the payroll. Pam Johnson of Macomb had completed her degree in this area so I hired her to take this position.

She was certainly a big help to me in planning our Labor Day celebration as she personally knew crafters from around the state. She knew of a crafter's guild in southern Illinois with a huge number of crafter members.

Don Powell had an old sorghum press that he offered to us for the show. We planted cane ahead of time so it would be ready to cut just before Labor Day. We also helped him make a large cook pan to cook down the sorghum.

George Myers talked the Trappy Ford Garage owner into letting us use his old sawmill. He had used this old sawmill to cut up trees he had cut out of Argyle Hollow when the park was developed.

Larry Buckert and Ed Powell set up the sawmill operation. They did an amazing job.

Floyd McClintock had been involved with gas engines and knew about the show. He owned a steam engine and loved showing it off. He offered to bring it out for the show. That really pulled things together as we could pull the sawmill with his steam engine as well as thresh grain the old-fashioned way.

I knew of a broom maker named Beckman from Augusta. He loved showing off his work at the Labor Day celebration. He would create his brooms while the visitors watched. He sold his brooms as well.

I also knew a potter named Don Copeland from Rushville. He would set up his pottery wheel so people could watch him create pottery. The crowd loved this. You could also purchase pieces from him.

My nephew, Gerald White, made apple butter using the copper kettle that had been in the family for over 100 years. This was a great attraction.

We also had someone making caramel corn in a big kettle.

Louise Myers of Macomb had made a lot of quilts that she loved to display.

There was a collection of toy farm equipment owned by John Lewis Pittenger to display.

A collection of barbed wire was a unique collection that attracted a lot of attention.

The guild had access to candle makers, basket weavers, bee keepers, whittlers and many more crafters that helped set the stage for a wonderful event. Pam contacted the guild and within a day we had all of the craft people we needed.

Mr. Gerald Redmond an antique dealer that I knew asked me if he could use the log cabin as a stocked replica of an Old Country Store. I was so excited. This certainly did fit in with our theme. We would make it happen.

Many local organizations, school groups, churches, and library, were able to make a lot of money during this celebration offering just a little bit of everything from lemon shake-ups, funnel cakes, corn dogs, onion rings, and much, much more.

It really made me feel good to see the youth of today interested in seeing and learning about the ways of the olden days.

SETTING UP ON FRIDAY

We had some old machines at the barn. I had the men start moving them to the show area. There was antique hay equipment, an old horse operated well drill, some old plows and an old-time thresher. People seemed to really enjoy looking at the farming methods of yesteryear.

Wendell Haines set up an eat tent for the weekend. He did as much business on Labor Day weekend as he did all year at the boat dock. He sold butterfly pork chops and ribeye sandwiches along with potato salad and baked beans. I helped him get a big electric line that ran directly from the shop.

Gerald White Stirring Apple Butter

The General Store

Erwin White Ranger White's Dad

A local church came in with an onion ring maker. The men of this church made this machine on wheels so that they could move it easily. I told them where to set up and then just left them alone.

The vendors were itching to get signed in, so I had my secretary, Dorothy McKee, come and help write vendor permits. We started at 12:30. There was a pretty good line until about 3 when we were finally caught up. Sign-up could be any time before 7pm. Otherwise they would have to wait until 7am on Saturday.

I went to the craft tent to make sure everyone had found their space. The broom maker and the potter would be in the same place as they were the previous year.

The antique dealer that setup his Old General Store in the log cabin needed a padlock and key. He had some valuable antiques on display in the store.

Some members of the gas engine club came and asked me if I had any corn knives. They wanted to cut the cane that we had planted in one of our fields. They wanted to get it cut and moved to the sorghum press area so that they would be ahead of the game for Saturday morning. I told them where the knives were and which wagon to use and they were on their way.

The Gas Engine Club sponsored the show and had people assigned to help line up the machinery by age and make.

I found myself running in every direction. People needed this and that. I did my best to help them all.

A local high school group wanted to know if they could use our 2-wheel trailer to haul water on. That was okay with me.

I ran into the President of the Gas Engine Club. I asked him if he was happy with where we had placed the bleachers for the show. He was happy and then apologized for not getting out to help earlier.

I realized it was about time for the men to go home and they should be at the shop. They were all watching steam engines being unloaded. I praised them for all the hard work they had done. I scheduled 2 men to work Saturday and 2 for Sunday.

I found a couple of problems with the vendors. One vendor who had told me that they would be selling their wares out of a small trailer but when they arrived, they had a big 5th wheel trailer! I had allowed enough space for a small trailer but not a big one. I looked at the schedule of vendors that were scheduled to be here on Saturday morning and did a little exchanging of spots.

There were also food vendors that needed large extension cords. I was able to fix them up.

My secretary, Dorothy, told me that she would stay until all the vendors had arrived. That was so good to hear because I was running around like a chicken with it's head cut off!

The Knights of Columbus found me and asked if they could move their tent about 5 feet from where I had it marked and they also needed some garbage barrels. I approved the move but held them off until morning on the barrels.

I suddenly panicked when I realized that the porta potties had not arrived! I rushed to my office to call and see where they were. His wife told me that he should be arriving here any minute. When I got back over to the show area he was there waiting for orders on where to place the 14 porta potties that I had ordered. It didn't take him long to get them all in place.

The men that had left to cut cane found me and wanted to use the tractor. The old one that they had planned to use wouldn't start. I reminded them to go ahead and be sure to take the hitch pin along because the wagon didn't have one.

It was crazy. People were everywhere setting up their areas and they all needed something from me.

Different vendors kept asking me for fuses. I got to them as soon as I could. I reminded everyone that they couldn't run air conditioners or any other heavy appliances because there were just too many people plugged in to the park's electrical source. They had to ration the electricity so that everyone could at least have lights. When I got to the shop to get the fuses, I decided that I could probably get around quicker if I drove the golf cart rather than getting caught in traffic. I loaded my cart with fuses, a tape measure, an axe, some rope, a flashlight and anything else I thought I might need.

On the Run

The ice man had his refrigerator trailer set up full of ice but no one had a key to get in. Everyone wanted that key! I just told them to go to the boat dock and get their ice until the ice man arrived with the key.

I had told Bette that she probably wouldn't see much of me for the next two days so be ready to go eat with me at a moments notice. It was getting time to eat and I was hungry, so while no one was after me we went to eat. We jumped in the truck and headed for the boat dock. We had just sat down with our sandwich when an irate couple found me. They were complaining about a camper next to them that had a non-stop barking dog. I asked if the dog was on a leash. They said that it was on a leash. I pacified him by telling him that when evening came I would come by and have the dog owner put their dog inside their trailer. This satisfied them enough to let me eat my sandwich.

HAPPY BIRTHDAY SMOKEY THE BEAR

Smokey the Bear had been a symbol of park safety for many years. The State of Illinois had a Smokey costume that was used for many kinds of events around the state. Months ago I had made a request to use the suit for the Labor Day Parade. It was Smokey's 40th birthday. My request was granted with many regulations. I had to verify that the person wearing the suit would not remove the head in public. There were other stipulations about size of person wearing the suit, conduct and positive attitude. My son-in-law, John Churchill, fit the criteria. He wore the suit and rode a 4-wheeler in the parade. He had a bucket of candy to throw out to the children. He said that it was un-BEAR-ably hot, but he made it!

Smokey the Bear

The gas engine and threshing machines were all in place. The flea marketers were all set up and ready to sell. The antique cars were all lined up for display.

Traffic was always heavy. People seemed to want to beat the crowds.

Sometimes flea marketers would have their tiffs, but that just happens when there are that many people.

There was an emergency phone call for a camper that had just signed in to camp. We found a copy of the permit that told us his location. They were in the overflow area. I had no idea where in the overflow. I did have a license number. Bette went with me to search for the plates. We finally found them sitting around the fire and we delivered the message. It wasn't easy but we found them.

I was required to go through the flea markets to make sure there was nothing illegal for sale. This took forever as it seemed everyone wanted to talk. Some even wanted to discuss their spot for next year.

We used radios to communicate for the next 3 days. I found it much easier to work my way through the crowds in my golf cart. I was running errands for everyone. I even delivered baby food jars to the apple butter tent.

I walked Agnes my burrow around and around at the sorghum press for a short time. She caught on very fast. I was getting some comments from the crowd like, "which one is the ass". It was all in fun.

During the 3 day event I had state troopers at the entrance to direct and park cars. This was sometimes a little tricky as not everyone wanted to park in the field and go to the celebration. Some were camping, some were fishing. We used the west field by the entrance to park cars. There were also people leaving. Traffic to town was unbelievable.

I often spelled the troopers so they could have a break. I ended up calling police headquarters for additional help. There were officers working traffic control in town Colchester as well.

Bette had received a call from the garbage people wondering if they should plan to make an extra run through the park each day. I called them back and told them YES!

My wife, Bette, had a collection of antique vinegar cruets. I knew if she wasn't at the house, she was walking through the flea markets looking for a new special cruet.

Wayne W. White

SATURDAY OF LABOR DAY WEEKEND

During Saturday's event I estimated 15,000 visitors at the show.

There would be a parade of cars and tractors every day at 1pm. They would also have a kiddy tractor pull.

Wade radioed me that he had received a call about a death in the family for a camper. He was going to take care of that.

My name was constantly being called over the intercom. Everyone needed something.

The porta potties needed attention. I radioed my men to do a porta potty run.

I stayed by the sawmill for a time and they let me saw a few logs. This was fun for me.

I noticed that the candle maker was letting each little kid make their own candle. I got involved in that for a while as well.

I took time to walk with Bette through the flea markets looking for more cruets.

I ran into one of my men who was on his way to replace a broken trampoline spring. I thanked heaven for all of the extra eyes watching for things like this.

Bette always bought a piece from the potter. This year he had made a special piece just for her. She was thrilled.

She also got a broom from the broom maker each year.

I couldn't wait to show Bette the General Store. She loved it.

Then we went by the quilt tent where our friend Louise Myers was showing off her quilting skills. She was upset because a dog had come through the tent and heisted it's leg on 2 of her best quilts. I didn't blame her one bit for being upset. Louise enjoyed telling people about the different stitches and patterns. I noticed that it was pretty dusty in her tent, so I had one of the men put some wood chips down to keep the dust from getting on her quilts.

When I took Bette back over to our house, my son, Dennis had just arrived. His wife, Cathy, was anxious to go seeking cobalt blue glassware. Dennis was wanting to look for baseball cards.

People were still calling for me to bring fuses, picnic tables, magic markers, and extension cords.

You could smell the delicious treats being sold in the show area.

You could hear the steam engines running. All of this created a special atmosphere. Other than meeting myself coming and going I loved it.

Back to the entrance I would go again to relieve the troopers for a bit. Just as I got out to the entrance an ambulance came with sirens wailing and lights flashing. I hadn't known of anyone needing an ambulance, but with so many people anything could happen. I soon learned that a man in the campground had had a heart attack. They loaded their patient up and away they went.

Toward evening Bette and I got a pork chop sandwich and listened to blue grass music. By 8pm three or four thousand cars had left the field.

When we went home Bette remarked to me to look at the stars. No rain for tomorrow. We've had years when it would come a downpour and it was a nightmare trying to get 1000's of people unstuck and out of the park. Fingers were crossed for this year.

My kids were all here. We sat outside in the front yard and visited. We could hear the blue grass music coming from the show area. I knew the music would quit at 9:30. After my kids left, Bette and I took a ride around the park. There really wasn't much activity on the other side of the park.

When my kids were all here during the celebration, we always had a big breakfast in the back yard. We had a huge skillet that could cook 2 dozen eggs at a time. We had a great time. There's nothing like family.

Family Breakfast

Wayne W. White

SUNDAY OF LABOR DAY WEEKEND

When I got up Sunday morning, all I could think of was PLEASE DON'T RAIN. At 6:30 it began to rain. I remembered the old saying; if it rains before 7 it will quit by 11. Flea marketers covered their wares with plastic. By 10am the rain had stopped and the sun was out. By gosh that old saying was true. The celebration continued and everything started all over again for another day. The plastic came off the tables and the flea marketers prepared for the final big day.

Thousands of people came to the park. My name was being called and I was on the run again.

The High School Music Boosters were serving breakfast, so I grabbed a quick bite.

I had the men get wood chips to put down in the wet areas where people were walking. Everyone appreciated our efforts.

I went by the library stand where they were making funnel cakes. There was a vat of hot grease setting at the edge of the tent. I was worried about a young child walking by and putting their hand in the hot grease. The library kids hadn't thought of that. I went and got a piece of plywood to put on top of the grease.

The exhibitors from a long way away packed up to leave in the early afternoon.

My kids were all getting ready to leave. I hadn't been able to spend much time with them but they understood. Dennis had about 180 miles to drive south. Cheryl had the same distance to the north. I promised my grandkids that winter was coming, and we would come and visit them.

At dark it was time for a ride around the park. On the far side of the park we came across a girl and boy walking down the road. When we stopped to see if they needed help, they asked for a ride to the entrance. The kids that they had been with had left them. They were going to see if they could catch a ride back to Macomb to the WIU campus. They climbed in the back of the truck and we delivered them to the entrance. They soon had a ride to Macomb.

We went in the house and went to bed. I was asleep before my head hit the pillow.

GAS ENGINE CLUB

The Gas Engine Club was formed by gas engine enthusiasts Frank Clark, Paul Powell and Raymond Cuba. This group of men came and asked me about having this Labor Day show. They wanted to show off their old time equipment. We had many discussions. I didn't want oil all over the area. We weighed all of the pros and cons and finally the Gas Engine Show was a go. We had no idea at the time how huge this event would become.

Sawmill

Sorghum Press

Threshing Machine

Boiling Sorghum

FALL

The Tuesday after Labor Day was an extremely busy day. Everything had to be cleaned up and everything returned to normal. I had a lot of bookwork to catch up on. The Labor Day celebration at Argyle seemed to me to be the closing of summer events. I looked forward to the beauty of fall at Argyle.

The students were back in school and camping had slowed down.

FIRE IN THE WOODS

Most all of the leaves had fallen from the trees. The R.O.T.C (Reserve Officers Training Corp) at Western University came to me seeking a place in the wilds for their students to have a bivouac to prepare for military situations that they might encounter later in their careers. They requested a wooded area. This operation took place on the next weekend. I hadn't foreseen that it would cause any problems with our park visitors. I certainly had no problem with them learning how to protect us someday.

This particular weekend my daughter, Cheryl, and her husband were visiting us from the Chicago area. On Sunday morning I took Duke, my son-in-law, to the boat dock for a big breakfast. When we had finished breakfast and were leaving, the R.O.T.C Captain came up to us with urgency. He needed help. The R.O.T.C students had been setting off flares in a war maneuver. The sparks from the flares had set the timber on fire! I told him that Duke and I would fill some backpack extinguishers and get to the area as soon as we could. He went with us and we filled the tanks with water and hurried to the area. We parked the truck and had to run the rest of the way to the fire. I had one backpack extinguisher and the Captain had the other. After we ran about a block, the Captain said to Duke "here, you carry this". Duke took the firefighter off his hands and we hurried on to the fire. I later told Duke, who was a Navy veteran, "10 years ago you would have said, "Yes Sir". Now, you could have said, "go to hell, but you didn't".

When we got there the young men were trying desperately to get the fire out. These kids were breathing the smoke and their eyes were burning. Some had to be taken back to the campus infirmary. It was quite an afternoon and evening before we got the fire out. There was about 100 acres that burned. We did get the fire put out and nothing was hurt. I felt that this might just be the last maneuver in Argyle Lake State Park.

ROAD RESURFACING

Our asphalt roads had been deteriorating for a few years and finally our turn had come for funding to be spent on Argyle roads. The contract was let to resurface all of the roads in the park. Coggeshall Construction of Clayton was awarded the contract because they had an asphalt plant in Macomb. I requested at the reconstruction conference that we wait until after our Labor Day celebration to begin the work. I also made a deal to make them close half the roads at a time while they were working on them. That eliminated the hiring of a flagman. The only thing that I demanded was that they not travel with loaded trucks over the finished mat. They agreed. They hadn't thought about what a problem that would be. They had to back up a long way with a loaded truck. I had worked with asphalt enough in my life to know that the heat of the new asphalt would bring moisture up under the old mat. I was proven right as there was one place where it just couldn't be done that way and sure enough, they had to redo that stretch because it broke up from the heavy loads. As one of the truck drivers was backing, he got too close to the edge of the road bed and slid off the side. He nearly went down a deep ravine. They got the auto patrol to pull him back onto the road. Another issue that they hadn't thought about was an asphalt spreader wouldn't have enough traction to pull up the hills after they applied the primer. This required a second truck to be hooked on to the spreader to pull it up the hill. It took about two weeks to complete this job. Boy was it ever nice to have good roads at Argyle again.

HELPING OUT A NEIGHBOR

A young man that lived near the park asked me if he could have some of the wooden slabs that were left by the saw mill. He said that he didn't have any money to pay for it but would work to pay for it. I told him that I really couldn't do that because of insurance but maybe he could help mow the entrance on Friday. He was as poor as a church mouse and needed wood for his families stove to keep warm. I was happy to help him and so were my men.

CLASS TRIPS IN THE FALL

Fall meant there would be a lot of schools bringing their 1st and 2nd graders out to the park for their nature study. I was used to a full schedule in the spring and the fall. When I got up this morning everything was wet and cloudy. The students from Table Grove school were scheduled to arrive at 9am for their walk through the woods.

As soon as the men came in to work, we decided it was too wet to mow so the best thing the men could do was continue cleaning up the area from the previous Labor Day weekend. Get trash into the barrels so the garbage truck could pick it all up. This garbage company that we used would not pick anything up off the ground. They only emptied the barrels. That is why I thought we could do the garbage pickup with our men as cheap as hiring it done. Not only that but it did cut into my contractual budget.

The phone rang and it was the teacher from Table Grove, wondering what she should do about coming over with the weather being so wet. I told her that if she wanted to come ahead, we would play it by ear and see what happened with the weather. I told her I wouldn't have any time the rest of the week as every day was scheduled. She decided since she had the bus scheduled, they would continue with their plan.

When they arrived, the weather had cleared and everything went well. I really enjoy these little kids as every experience was a new experience to them. I felt that after the 3rd grade most of the kids were just getting a day away from the classroom and weren't too interested. They would want to run ahead and not listen to my speech. The younger ones though were very interested. I would see an old log laying along the trail and I would ask if that old log was any good for anything, and of course they said no. When I moved the logs lot of bugs ran out from under it to seek shelter someplace else. Then I would ask again if the log was any good for anything and usually they would answer the same as before until I reminded them that the bugs that lived under the log were God's creatures and they needed a place to live just like we do. Their little mouths would fall open as they thought about it. I would find some poison ivy along the trail and I would make sure they knew what it was before the day was over. My saying was; *Leaves of Three, Let it Be.* Still today when I see some of those students who have grown up, they still say to me, *Leaves of Three, Let it Be.* I also always made the statement; *Take only Memories and Leave Only Footprints.* It amazed me that these grown up kids still remember. It must have made an impression on their little minds. I had a stuffed badger and rabbit in my office to show them and let them touch. These trips usually took about an hour or two and they would have enough time to eat their lunches that they had brought and a still had time to play on the playground before leaving for home.

By the time I was finished with the school kids the grass had dried off and the seniors went to mow.

There were class trips scheduled for everyday for a while.

WHAT WERE THEY DOING?

Friday night was the first weekend after the return of the students, it was pretty hectic. When I approached a party in the south woods it appeared that they were having some kind of ritual. There were four fires and fraternity pledges that were doing something by each fire. I told them it was time to wrap it up and leave. They complied.

MAKE ME SMILE

About three weeks after Labor Day Gordy Taylor and his fraternity brothers came out to Argyle and asked me about the possibility of having an all university party called "Make Me Smile" to benefit the Crippled Children Program. They explained that they were planning to have a battle of the bands that would include four different bands. They would charge each student for this party. They had arranged a deal with the beer company to furnish the drinks at a reduced rate. I decided that most of those university students would probably be here anyway so with the fraternity offering to have police here for any problem that might come up it seemed a good arrangement. The only problem that I could see was that they would have to find a way to charge the students before they came to the park as this would be a concession conflict. They felt that they could handle that problem. They wanted to have this bash the first Saturday night in October. That was okay with me.

And so it happened, the biggest crowd of college kids ever was at Argyle. Gordy Taylor had found a way to charge the kids as I had requested. The pre-paid students would have a stamp on their hand. Gordy told me that on Saturday, nearly all of the university students were going to be here!

Saturday morning came and the first to show up was the beer truck with the drinks for the day. Next came a couple of Delta Sigs to ask for some steel posts to set up lines to the kegs. I found 8 steel posts and some rope. They made their lines to the kegs. The fraternity had borrowed a flatbed trailer to use as a stage for the bands. They got the trailers close enough to reach electricity for their amps.

The students started showing up at 12:30 ready for a full afternoon of fun. The auxiliary police showed up but as luck would have it, they were not needed all day.

The State of Illinois had been experimenting with age limits for voting and alcohol consumption. They had lowered the drinking age to 18. After one year the State decided that they could not leave the legal drinking age at 18. The age limit went back to 21 years of age. They left the voting age at 18.

This meant that most politicians would be working the college campuses often. A man named Scott was running for Attorney General of Illinois. A celebrity by the name of Arthur Godfrey was helping with his campaign. They just happened on the WIU campus on this Saturday to campaign but found that the WIU campus was like a ghost town. The students were all at Argyle Lake State Park for the "Make Me Smile" party. They couldn't pass up a chance to see this many students altogether in one setting. They came to Argyle and hit the jackpot. Mr. Scott positioned himself at the front of one of the beer lines drawing beer for students all afternoon.

It was unbelievable! There was a sea of young people completely covering the pines area.

Bette just loved it because she got to visit with Arthur Godfrey all afternoon. Can you guess... Mr. Scott got elected.

At 4:30 all of the music stopped and all students left to go back to campus. There were so many that it took both lanes going into Colchester.

The following week my wife and I were invited to the Delta Sig house for dinner. While there we watched the Delta Sigs present a check for $1800. to the Crippled Children Program. At the dinner the Delta Sig President told me that 101 kegs of beer were consumed at the "Make Me Smile" event without any problems at all.

A ONE TIME SQUARE DANCE

Wendell asked me to use some picnic tables at the boat dock. He wanted to try and serve catfish outside. He wanted to try an experiment by having music and square dancing. We got him the tables. Everything was planned except for someone to call the square dance. He asked me to call the square dance. That I did but there just wasn't enough interest in the dancing so he did not continue this.

THE LOST RING

One Sunday evening, a sorority was having a weiner roast in the picnic area nearest my home.

They had raked up a really large pile of leaves and they were having a ball throwing each other into the leaves. One of the freshman girls lost her class ring that her parents had just given her before she had left home to come to Western. She came over to my house just as I was getting out of my truck. She was concerned that we would be moving the leaves tomorrow. She wanted to come out tomorrow and look for her ring. I told her that I might be able to help her out. I had just purchased a metal detector for my wife. I went right in the house and asked my Bette if she would come and try out her new toy. She was excited to try it out. We all went over to the leaf pile. Within 10 minutes of detecting over the leaves, we found the girls ring! She was so happy. They all went back to campus with one very relieved young lady.

PULLING THE PLUG

Saturday and another university party. One of the fraternities along with their sister sorority had hired a band called MORNING MORNING to play for a dance in the picnic area where the VFW was to have their annual picnic the next day. The VFW had set up their tent in case of bad weather. A couple of VFW members stayed all night so they could begin cooking early in the morning. This band was well known around the area and were really pretty good. They lived at the old Vishnu Springs Hotel during the week. It was just before 10pm when I went by and told them that this would have to be their last song. Quiet time was upon us and the students would have to leave the park. I went back to my station and heard them start up another song. I went back over and told them to wrap it up. They told me, "Ok", so I started back to my station. They started up another song, so I walked back to the electric source and pulled out all of the amplifier cords. The music went silent and I just stood there by the electrical outlets. There was a really big kid that wanted to intimidate me. He came over to me and said "you better not have ruined our amps". Finally, after I stood there for awhile, they started rolling up their cords to leave. I walked over just a few feet to the VFW tent where the two guys had just seen what had happened. They said to me, "man, you have to have a lot of nerve to call their bluff like that". I told them that those kids would have played all night if I hadn't stood my ground.

ANOTHER RUGBY TOURNAMENT

It was Saturday and there was a Rugby Tournament planned. The goal posts were set so they could play 4 games at a time.

I had fed the animals and ran the toilets before 9am. There weren't many fishermen so I decided to go watch some rugby.

The teams were all there and ready. There were 12 teams in all from Chicago, Wisconsin, Indiana, Ohio, and Iowa. There were two teams from W.I.U. At 11am they got two games started. I had never seen this game played before. I didn't see how they kept from killing each other. The team that had the ball was free game. You could kick it or roll it forward. They had to pass it lateral or backward. When a team member had the ball in his hand, there would be a dogpile. Lots of injuries in this game.

When I returned to the office, there were two law enforcement officers that came by, so I suggested that they go over to the rugby games and put a stop to the drinking. They laughed and said, "No way". When I would find someone drinking, I just checked their age and then poured it out. They didn't like it much but it was better than being arrested. When the tournament was over, they all headed for Macomb to party.

There were two parties planned for that evening. One of the fraternity cars was a hearst. The fraternity boys told me it was called THE MAYLOWER because they said, "more girls came across on it". Oh my.

I was supposed to get some law enforcement help this weekend.

As usual on Saturday night, we ate supper cooked over an open fire at the check in station. Only one policeman showed up. We invited him to eat with us. He wanted to take a drive around the park first. When he returned, he reported that there were three different congregations partying on the other side of the park. I told him that I would usually go run them out at 10pm. He said the he had to leave at 9. That wasn't surprising.

A band had started up while we were eating. The officer could not believe all of the traffic and that we had so many students all at once. He rode with me to some of the parties so that he could get acclimated to the area. He finally left and the four of us headed around the park. One of the parties had kids scattered all throughout the woods on blankets. When our truck lights lit on them, they hurriedly jumped up and put their pants on. They really didn't seem to mind who saw them. We managed to get everyone up and out of there.

Sunday morning the local scavenger hunters looked to see what the kids had left behind the night before. Sometimes they would find things like blankets and radios. Too bad for me that they didn't pick up the beer cans. I always tried to get the picnic areas cleaned up first. I wanted everything presentable for the reunions and other people having picnics.

ARCHERY RANGE

While I was picking up garbage, a couple of fellows approached me to see what needed to be done to make our archery range usable again. I agreed to fix the paths and bridges near the range if they would take care of the targets. We spent quite a bit of time inspecting the area. They wanted to provide 14 targets so that they could have sanctioned events. I thought this was a great idea. I told them that I needed to get state approval, but I didn't foresee any problems.

PONTOON JUMPERS

It was Sunday noon and traffic had started to pick up. I caught some big kids climbing on top of pontoons. I made them stop. It was quite warm and I was used to kids wanting to swim. In the early afternoon there they were back on top of the pontoons. This time however, they were drinking and throwing the girls in the water. I was finally able to get that stopped with the threat of arrest.

A SIGN FOR THE DORM

On the park closing ride I found a boy who was struggling to get a sign in his trunk. I pulled up behind him and he yelled for me to shine my lights so he could see. I did this and when he looked up and saw that it was me, he almost dropped to his knees. It was one of our parking signs. He was stealing it to take back to his dorm room. He begged with all of his might. He cried, "I'm just a freshman, I didn't know any better, I'm on the baseball team, I will get in so much trouble". Kindly I told him that I would be issuing him a citation and he could pay his fine without WIU being involved. He accepted the consequences.

On Monday I took two of my men to the archery range area. I explained the plans to them so they would be able to start cleaning up the area and moving logs in to build bridges.

While they were busy doing that, I had weekend bookwork to do.

While at the office I received a call from a high-ranking state official who had visited the Labor Day celebration. He was calling to compliment me on a spectacular event. It made my day.

I went into town to deposit the camping receipts. I decided I might as well drop by and visit my barber, Mike Biswell, and get a haircut. He was always fun to argue with.

I was back at the park before the men left. They told me that they were missing the C.E.T.A workers. I did too.

PUBLIC SERVICE

On Tuesday I received a call from a local Judge in the county seat. He wanted to know if I could use some help. That was music to my ears. He told me that he would be sentencing a young fellow to 100 hours of public service. He would send him my way. All I had to do was keep the court apprised of his progress. This was such a good way to deal with young offenders.

I got another call about a 3rd grade field trip.

I had just hung up when a couple came in my office requesting the use of the chapel.

The floating docks were full of sun bathers. Kids were renting boats. It was probably the last warm weekend.

RIVER RIDE

I decided to take a day off and take Bette and go for a ride over to the Mississippi River just to get away for a little while. We watched the barges pass through the new locks. I thought it was really interesting. We drove on up the river road and had a nice dinner at Nauvoo. I must have needed a break because I really enjoyed myself.

The last part of September meant lots of parties. The weather is beautiful and the students want to get their fill before winter.

There was a trail ride coming up soon so I walked the entire trail to be sure it was all safe.

TROUT RELEASE

It was now the beginning of October. I had ordered trout for the lake and they were to be delivered this week. I contacted the local newspaper and radio station. When the fish arrived, they came out and took photos of the release. There was a large crowd of people that came to watch.

The fall colors were just at their peak. I expected a lot of traffic over the weekend. People would come to Argyle just to enjoy driving around the park admiring the beautiful trees.

Friday was a particularly busy night. It seemed that the kids were to cram in all the fun they could before winter. Some kids brought hot dogs and marshmallows while others just wanted beer. I know someone could have made a fortune selling weenie sticks. Parties got pretty loud. I tried to put them over in the south woods where they didn't disturb anyone.

When I did the 10 o'clock runs, I was now carrying a back pack fire extinguisher in the back of the truck to put out fires when they left. It took a while but it was worth it to make sure the campfires were out and the kids were on their way.

Wade remarked to me that there were no stars. You remember that that usually meant rain. I was disappointed when the rain made the beautiful leaves fall. The next morning it was raining and the leaves were falling. I did my chores with a rain suit on.

FISHING DERBY

There were a lot of boat trailers lined up at the docks for a 2-day fishing derby. Rain didn't hinder the fishermen who loved to fish. They would keep their catch alive and set their fish free after weighing them. There were clubs of fishermen that competed.

Monday was the first day that trout fishing was allowed. People were out before 6am to catch their 5 fish limit. Some used corn for bait while others used worms. When I went to the boat dock to get my morning coffee there were 30 people fishing. I enjoyed watching until it was time for my men to arrive and I had to leave.

TURKEY RELEASE

The game biologist came out to discuss a turkey release at Argyle. He planned to trap turkeys in the southwest corner of the county and bring them to Argyle for release. The game biologist had been watching these birds for a while. He needed help trapping the turkeys. He set a net in the afternoon and I took one of my men and went to help early in the morning. We caught 19 turkeys. The biologist brought them to the park and released them. They seemed a little dazed. They didn't take off running right away, but they would be okay.

Squirrel hunters told me of scaring up turkeys during their hunt. The release of turkeys in the park hadn't been disclosed yet so the hunters were surprised.

We took the stove pipe down in the maintenance building to clean and prepare it for winter. Some of the pipes were rusty so we just replaced them.

It was about 11pm and I was ready to retire for the night when a motor home pulled in and wanted to camp. They had come down from Chicago to pick up their son at the university. I was happy to show them a good place to set up.

It turned out to be a rainy weekend. I cleaned out the animal pens and then Bette and I went to the docks and watched a group of old people that had been brought out from a nursing home fishing for trout. These old people had ball. I loved this. Times like this made everything worthwhile.

We went for a ride in the patrol boat. I wanted to check on the compressor at the tower before winter. We also checked for beaver activity in a far finger of the lake. The beavers had cut almost every tree along the east bank of this finger. Beavers can destroy a shoreline very quickly. They had been a problem this year. I hoped they would not return.

It was to freeze this night so Bette and I moved her plants inside. While we were doing this a car drove into the playground area and began spinning his tires and cutting donuts. I took off in a dead run to stop him. He nearly ran over me. He was headed for an opening, I yelled at Wade, who was in the check-in station to "STOP THAT CAR"! Wade ran to the middle of the road and tried to halt this crazy driver by waving his flashlight at him. It became evident that he was not going to stop, so Wade stepped back and threw his flashlight at the car window as he sped past. He got away but Wade thought he had broken the glass window. The next day I went up to the university dorms and drove around to see if I could spot this car. I never found it.

HERMIT IN THE WOODS

A hunter pulled up to the shop to tell me that during his walk far back in the woods he had come upon an old ragged tent that appeared as though someone was living there. I decided that I had better check out this area and see if I could find the tent. I found the tent and met up with a man who looked to be in his 30's. Apparently he had not bathed in a very long time. I questioned him to try and find out why he was a squatter here. He told me that he was fed up with life and just wanted to exist alone as a hermit. I had to tell him that even though he wasn't hurting a thing he would have to clear out by the end of the week. He seemed confused but he did honor the message.

HAYRACK RIDE

Late October at about noontime some college girls came out and asked about having a hayrack ride during the upcoming weekend. They wanted me to provide the hayrack, the hay, the tractor, and the driver! It was comical to me but I aimed to please. I chose one my single men to take care of this little project. I had him pick up a few bales of hay for the girls to sit on. He got the hayrack out and cleaned it all up and aired the tires up on the tractor. He was to meet the girls in the pines at 7pm. The hayride went really well. The girls had a lot of fun.

Word travelled quickly and more kids were requesting hayrides.

Wendell told me that he was going to close down the concession stand for the winter and would be open only on weekends for a while. It was a good idea. Business had slowed way down. I could handle any boat rental requests that might arise.

The weather was nice so I used this day to walk the foot trails. I did this from time to time to make sure that the paths were free of fallen limbs. I also checked the condition of the bridges. It was enjoyable. I realized that some of these trails needed to be marked better. A stranger to the area would have trouble following the route. By noon I had walked the 4 ½ miles of trails and had written down a lot of needed repair work. When the men arrived on Monday, I gave them my list and we discussed more signage. The grass had pretty much quit growing so they would have time to do these repairs.

HALLOWEEN PARTY

A group of college boys came to my office and wanted to let me know of a Halloween party that they were planning. It was to be attended by all of the fraternities and sororities. I gave my approval with the stipulation that they would all be gone by 10pm. They wanted to build a very large bon fire. I directed them to the best place for their gathering. While the party was going on, I checked on them several times. They were having a blast; they were cooking weenies and marshmallows. They of course had beer and cider. They had lots of fun and gave me not a bit of trouble. By 10:30 they were all gone.

NOVEMBER 1ST

The entrance to the park was looking kind of ragged. I had the men do some spot mowing. I spent the morning putting up bird feeders. Bette was busy picking up hickory nuts. She would crack these nuts and pick the nutmeats out. She used them in her famous hickory nut cake. She always sent some to her brother in California.

November 4 brought a pretty hard freeze.

I ran into a man at the docks and he wanted to know if I would like to have an old race car for the playground area. There were no axles and no engine. In my mind I could picture it all painted up with kids climbing in it pretending to drive. We went and got it right then. I would have it ready for the play area by spring.

The men were busy cleaning and winterizing our equipment. They built a few duck houses to scatter around. It was time to start hauling picnic tables into the maintenance area. There were about 600 tables in the park. The men made rows according to what needed to be done to them. Some needed extensive repair, some needed a small amount of repair and others just needed painting. We would work on these repairs all winter long.

I drained the water lines in the campgrounds, hung some duck houses and went in the house to watch a football game.

For dinner we went to Tennessee to my sister Juanita's house. We played some cards and were home by 10.

The men spent the next day raking in the picnic areas. The weatherman was beginning to report the possibilities of snow.

I took Bette to a bingo game at the American Legion hall. We ate there and played bingo all evening. Bette won enough to pay for our evening.

I checked the chapel area and discovered that some of the benches had been broken up for firewood. It's a kind of vandalism that I found very hard to take. I had the men replace the broken benches right away.

TRAIL RIDE

On Saturday November 16th the Saddle Club had their last trail ride. They invited me to join them. I rode a horse belonging to Van Edison. The horse's name was "Pawnee". I really enjoyed this as well as becoming aware of the needs of the trail riders.

November 20th it was 20°. Our day was spent winterizing the concession area. There was a thin layer of ice beginning to form on the lake.

We made sure there was plenty of straw for the animals.

Pontoon owners are beginning to remove their pontoon boats, they are supposed to have them out by December 1st.

THANKSGIVING

Bette and I enjoyed Thanksgiving Dinner at my sister Juanita's house in Tennessee.

There was no work on Thanksgiving. Two of my men had requested Friday off as well.

DEER SEASON

Deer season was the weekend before and the weekend after Thanksgiving. The deer hunting reporting station was set up in the Argyle maintenance building. Three college kids were hired to open for check-ins at 7 am. They knew how to age and sex the deer for the state statistical information. The hunters began coming in soon after opening. By 4 pm, 104 deer had been reported. It was dark before the largest surge of hunters came in to register their kill. I set up two large flood lights to light the area so they could see what they were doing.

Bette went to town and bought pizzas for those working the deer station. They were all thrilled. There had not had a chance to eat anything since early morning.

The line of hunters backed up until about 7pm when they were finally caught up. The final count for this first day of deer hunting was 238.

Saturday was another good day for the hunters. The temperature was just at freezing and the sun was shining. The deer count for Saturday was 188.

Sunday, the last day of the first deer hunting season had a count of 110.

On December 1st it got down to 15°. When I got up, I went to the maintenance building to start a fire and make coffee before the men arrived.

I picked up some pine limbs and greens to make grave blankets for our parent's graves.

The lake was getting frozen. There were still 3 pontoons that had not been removed. I wasn't going to worry too much about this because I was busy and because I was not in agreement with the pontoon removal rule.

I made sure barricades were ready to put up to prevent people from trying to drive around the park.

Bette had started Christmas shopping. She would go shopping with her sisters, Leola Simmons and Ella Mae Waddill. They always had a good time together.

On Friday, December 12th, we woke up to 5 inches of snow on the ground. I liked blading snow, so I had our entrance and the road to our house and the maintenance building cleaned off in short time. This weekend was the 2nd deer hunting season.

The sun shining on the snow in the pine trees was just beautiful. I got my camera and took pictures. I thought to myself that it was time to start seeing snowmobiles.

I would drive up and down sledder's hill several times to pack the snow down for those who came to coast.

About 50 college kids came out to coast down the hill on cafeteria trays they had borrowed from their food service. They also tried to use our row boats. I put a stop to that immediately. Some snowmobiles came out and I warned them to be watchful of those coasting. Coasters young and old loved sledding down the boat dock hill.

It was Sunday, December 14th. Bette reminded me that there was only one week remaining until Christmas. We HAD to go shopping. Bette wanted to get the grandchildren Cabbage Patch dolls. They were extremely hard to find. This made her even more determined. We always bought our grandchildren gifts and gave our own kids money. We always had fun coming up with unique ways to present the money. One time we put it in a golden spittoon type pot with a little pine tree planted on top. This year I purchased three monopoly games. I steamed them open and replaced the play money with real money and sealed them shut.

We bought sleds for the little boys, Carhartt coats for the bigger boys and outfits from Suzie's for the girls.

We bought big red bows for the grave blankets.

It was hard to get shopping done because it seemed that everyone knew me and wanted to stop and talk.

When we got home, I watched a football game and Bette wrapped presents.

We went to my sister's house for dinner.

When we returned home, I noticed a bonfire in the pines. It was a fraternity having a party.

The next day the men wanted a break from painting. They put up boundary signs. They had all winter to paint.

Wednesday morning when the men came to work they found all kinds a food and goodies, a couple of the men's wives came out as well as mine and we had a little Christmas party. They partied until about 3 when I told them Merry Christmas, go home and I would see them all next Monday. They were excited to have 5 days off.

On Christmas morning we woke up to 2 inches of snow. Christmas morning is for kids, but before we could go into our daughter's house, I would have to feed the animals and birds.

Our daughter, JoAnne, had our family's Christmas celebration. All of our kids and their families were there. We ate and enjoyed each other all day. Everyone had a grand time. After eating too much, some took naps while the rest of us played Monopoly!

About 8:30 Bette and I decided to call it a day a returned home to Argyle.

On December 26th we pieced on all of the goodies that JoAnne had sent home with us. At about 11am Dennis came out and wanted to go rabbit hunting. The girls all headed to the Macomb Hallmark store to the ½ price sales. Later in the afternoon we all loaded up and went to the Italian Village for pizza.

The next day Dennis and his family and Cheryl and her family headed for their homes. The weather was beginning to get bad. Bette and I watched a movie called Trains, Planes and Automobiles that was a Christmas gift. We loved it. The snow kept coming and by dark we had about 6 inches on the ground with no sign of it stopping.

During the snowy winter days there were many snowmobiles and sled riders.

I had my men build animal pens in the barn so we could get the animals in out of the weather. The birds needed plenty of food.

I completed many end-of-the-year reports.

MY YEAR IS COMPLETE

A year in my life from January 1st through December 31st is now complete. My year as a Park Ranger was, fun, hectic, stressful and exciting. Each day brought a new adventure. Most of all it was fulfilling to know that I had played an important role in providing and maintaining a safe, enjoyable, and beautiful environment for the visitors of Argyle Lake State Park.

THE CREATION OF ARGYLE LAKE STATE PARK

In 1947, the State of Illinois had a Republican Governor named Green. His popularity was not high enough to get re-elected. The party needed to boost his electability status for the coming year. Being in control of state government they had the ability to manipulate government funds. They knew that the Conservation Department had quite a sum of money attained from the sale of fishing and hunting licenses and fines. It was thought that if they were to spread this money around the state by building conservation areas it might change the feelings of enough voters to get Governor Green re-elected. They thought there was enough money to build 13 of these areas all over the state. As it turned out there was only enough funds for 3. Hunting and sportsman clubs were asked to send in proposals so the engineers could study their plans as well as their help in the region where they could gain the most votes.

During the next few weeks and months there was a lot of politicking and hand shaking going on by different groups trying to get a conservation area in their region. Many trips were made to Springfield to try and influence the decision.

McDonough County came in first among all the proposals as they had a sight where 4000 acres of watershed went through a very small pass of only 800 feet, with a rock structure ideal for the building of a dam. Opposition was keen as McDonough County did not have a lot of voters and the county was already leaning Republican. The land proposed was very poor and could be purchased at a reasonable price which was a factor in the state's decision. Against powerful opposition the McDonough County site was selected for one of the sites. The other 2 sites selected were Murphysboro Lake and Ramsey Lake. Both of these areas were in southern Illinois.

The area selected for this ideal construction site was north of Colchester where most of the occupants of this area came from Argyle England. They called this area Argyle Hollow. From that the name Argyle Lake State Park was given.

When the news came out that Argyle Hollow had been selected, local people were very excited. West Central Illinois didn't usually get much attention due to the low population. The state was in a big hurry to get the land purchased and get the dam started. Time was running out to help the governor get re-elected. The state sent appraisers, surveyors, and agents to locate the land parcels and their owners. The people who owned the land parcels hardly knew where their boundaries were. Today good records are kept even in the hills of the land. As the legal land owners were recognized the purchasing agents were right there to purchase the land. These parcels were so small that they ended up purchasing from 29 different people. In 1967, I discovered that 1/3 of an acre right in the middle of the park had never been purchased. I was able to get payment for the owner of this parcel.

The state engineers wanted the trees to be removed where the water was to be. The contract was let out to different contractors. One was to build the dam and one to remove the trees and another to build the roads within the site. John McClure had the task of building the roads on this very rough terrain. John owned a local rock quarry and had the equipment to do the work. Mr. Trapp who owned the local Ford garage in Macomb had a sawmill. He was given the job of removing the trees. He hired area people to do the cutting and sawing. The state was in a hurry to get the Conservation Area built. They had spent too much time in the site selection.

Local men worked on the project. Bus Wayland was a carpenter and helped build the drain tower which would be out in the middle of the lake. Herb Roberts worked for Mr. Trapp cutting the trees. Speed Yard ran earth moving equipment building the dirt dam. There were many others involved. The Forestry Department came to plant trees. The foresters were asked to work 10 hours a day, 7 days a week. I don't know who decided where each species of trees were to be planted but it appeared that no one did much planning as they would plant one row of pines and the next row would be hardwoods. There were a lot of pines, black locusts, and sycamores planted in the same areas. The pines could not compete with the hardwoods resulting in a lot of pines dying from lack of sunlight.

The following is a list of original land purchases:
William Duncan .... 35 acres .... $2,025.
T. Mack Downing .... 40 acre .... $3,025.
Ralph Creasey .... 2.27 acres ....
Clyde Calvert .... 10 acres .... $ 750.
Samuel Bishop .... 10 acres .... $ 475.
Ralph Creasey .... 20 acres .... $1,025.
Annie Martin .... 43 acres .... $1,825.
+ her 11 children ....
Charles Creasey .... Improvements on the land
                               $10. per acre .... $2,025.
Allie Vawter .... 21 acres .... $2,113.
Robert Elder .... 40 acres .... $2,500.
Homer Hoyt .... 40 acres .... $2,500.
Robert Miller .... 150 acres .... $6,850.
Benjamin McGrann .... 31.29 acres .... $1,301.
Billie Jones .... 53 acres .... $4,000.
Lucy Worley .... 40 acres .... $2,525.
Hughey Martin .... 193 acres .... $12,440.
Henry Vawter .... 3.75 acres .... $ 325.

Alice McCord .... 1 acre .... $5.
George Huff .... 40 acres .... $1,225.
Lloyd Hall .... 29 acres .... $2,055.
Emma Mustain .... 38 acres .... $2,000.
Damon Mustain .... 1 1/5 ac .... $1.
Charles Creasey .... 20.66 acres .... $1,150.
Hughey Martin .... 51 acres .... $7,650.
Thomas Baumgardner.. 10 acres .... $ 400.
Elmer Justice .... 50 acres .... $2,000.

Total cost of land to be used: $ 70,500.

This land today would bring far more. I believe all land owners were happy with the sale of their land.

ARGYLE LAKE STATE PARK DEDICATION 1949

New Dam

MY RETIREMENT

IN 1991, I decided it was time for me to retire and leave the management of Argyle Lake State Park to the next generation. I was given the most wonderful retirement celebration. My 3 children planned a huge event at the park. Over 500 people attended.

There was food and quite a spectacular program. My son, Dennis, was the Master of Ceremonies. There were performances by the Colchester High School vocal and instrumental music groups. The WIU Jazz Band played. A hysterically funny skit about a hiker at Argyle was performed by local friend and teacher, Julie Bice. Presentations were made by teacher Ruth Sibley, Duane Beck, Gordy Taylor, Representative Bill Edley, and Conservation Department Officials. A very special presentation was made my 6 grandchildren.

It was so awesome. Many times I have thought that I left too soon. I missed being at Argyle terribly.

Teacher Julie Bice

Teacher Ruth Sibley

Gordy Taylor

```
        Dedicated to RANGER WAYNE WHITE
            for 25 Years of Service


    YOU HAVE TOUCHED MANY LIVES IN TWENTY-FIVE YEARS,
    THE CHILDREN OF CHILDREN, THE LAUGHTER...THE TEARS,
    YOU HAVE SERVED AS OUR GUIDE, OUR TEACHER, OUR FRIEND,
       OPENED A WORLD OF FANTASY AROUND EVERY BEND.
  NOW EACH PATH THAT WE FOLLOW, EACH FLOWER'S BRILLIANT HUE,
       WILL ALWAYS CONJURE TENDER MEMORIES OF YOU.
      YOU'VE TAUGHT US THE LESSONS OF WONDER AND PLEASURE,
    TO RESPECT "MOTHER NATURE" ... GOD'S PRECIOUS TREASURE.
    THE CHILDREN, AND THEIR CHILDREN, HAVE GATHERED TODAY,
       TO HONOR AND THANK-YOU ... "THE WIZARD OF PLAY!"


                      With Love,
            The Children and Staff of Colchester Unit #180


      "Take only memories....
          Leave only footprints"



                   APRIL 28, 1991
```

A FAMILY MESSAGE

97 year old Wayne White has spent his entire life in service to others. With an undying commitment to his family, his community, his country, and his faith, his life has been full. Now, he wants to share some experiences of his life.

In his first book, IT WASN'T MY TIME, he reflects on the harrowing experiences he encountered during WWII as a member of the 15th Air Force.

In 1966, he began a new career as a State Park Ranger in Illinois. Located near Western Illinois University, the park was a retreat for thousands of college kids. For Wayne there was never a dull moment. In this book, A YEAR IN MY LIFE AS A PARK RANGER, he gives a seasonal description of what a year was like for him as the Ranger at Argyle Lake State Park.

We hope you enjoy reading his book as much as he enjoyed writing it.

Wayne and Bette White

A SPECIAL THANK YOU

I want to thank everyone who helped me make this book. I'm sure I cannot name each one. The encouragement I received was extraordinary. I thank my three kids; Dennis White, Cheryl White Krauspe, and JoAnne White Churchill. I thank those I received photos from to include Janet Sowers, Kathy Numberg, Gordy Taylor, Tom Stites, Julie Bice, and my dear friend Larry Louderman.

ABOUT THE AUTHOR

At 97 years old, Wayne White, has spent his entire life in service to others. With an undying commitment to his family, his community, his country, and his faith, his life has been full. Now, he wants to share some experiences of his life.

In his first book, IT WASN'T MY TIME, he reflects on the harrowing experiences he encountered during WWII as a member of the 15th Air Force.

After his time in WWII, he returned home to his wife, Bette, and together they raised three children.

He worked in construction for many years building Illinois highways.

In addition to his work he was involved in many things such as basketball referee, auctioneer, baseball umpire, Lions Club member and member of the Christian Church, to name a few.

In 1966, he began a new career as a Illinois State Park Ranger. Located near Western Illinois University, Argyle Lake State Park was a retreat for thousands of college kids. For Ranger White, there was never a dull moment. In this book, ARGYLE... A YEAR IN MY LIFE AS A PARK RANGER, he gives a seasonal description of what an entire year was like for him as the Ranger at Argyle Lake State Park.

CPSIA information can be obtained
at www.ICGtesting.com
Printed in the USA
LVHW030348011220
673036LV00006B/1051